That Reminds Me of a
STORY...

A Rare Collection by
Gayle D. Erwin

That Reminds Me of a Story
Copyright C 1997 by Gayle D. Erwin
Printed in the United States of America
ISBN 1-56599-252-0

YASHUA Publishing
PO Box 219
Cathedral City, CA 92235-0219
Phone (760) 321-0077
Fax (760) 202-1139

Table of Contents

Let Me Explain

...Jesus spoke to the multitudes in parables; and without a parable he did not speak to them. Matthew 13:34 NKJ

Every person I ever met was a book waiting to be written. Usually, I had opportunity only to read a phrase, occasionally a sentence, rarely a paragraph, miraculously a chapter. This is a book of phrases from my life and people I have met. For me, a joy of Heaven will be to "know as I am known." In Heaven, I finally get to read the whole book of the life of everyone there. In the meantime, I get glimpses of Heaven with only an occasional shudder of Hell.

The stories you are about to read are true. Occasionally names and locations are changed or omitted for obvious reasons. Every story has a point, a moral, a lesson—sometimes blatant, sometimes subtle. Because there is a point and because some might want to use these in group or family meetings, each story has applicational questions at the end for discussion or private consideration.

These stories, written because those who heard me tell them demanded, result from the incredible life God has given me. In the compressed and intensified experiences of my allotted years, I learned a lot, laughed a lot, cried a lot. As you read these, I hope you will also learn, laugh and cry, and, at the same time, remember the stories in your own life, the stuff of which parables are made.

And this is only the beginning.

The Runner

My father was a pastor. At one point in his ministry, he began taking flying lessons at a nearby community airport in order to go into the interior of the state to begin some additional churches. Once, while at the airport for a lesson, a military training plane from a nearby airbase landed there. That landing violated military regulations.

The pilot got out and chatted with my dad and the others there. He asked my dad, "Have you ever flown in a training plane?"

"No."

"Would you like to?"

"Sure!"

"Hop in."

He wasn't supposed to ask my dad and my dad wasn't supposed to get in, but he did and he did. This errant pilot did not use adequate runway to take off. He managed to get airborne but was unable to clear some trees beyond the runway. He clipped the top of them and the plane crashed.

Life was changed for everybody at that moment. The pilot was not severely injured, but my father was–his brain badly damaged and his left side paralyzed. The Air Force, dictated by military discipline, moved to throw the pilot in prison for twenty-five years. My father, who was cut from different cloth, went to bat for the pilot and pleaded with the Air Force not to be so hard on the pilot since he had boarded the plane voluntarily. So, the Air Force issued the pilot a dishonorable discharge which is severe enough in itself.

We were penniless, so my parents approached the Air Force to see if they could help us. Their response? "We are not responsible, because this man was not doing Air Force duty when this accident occurred. We may prosecute you for getting in the plane if you don't leave us alone."

Now, this became a civil liability case. The pilot was responsible and he knew that, so he disappeared. My parents began a year-long hunt with government help to find him. (This was before the days of computers–they know where you are now!)

After locating him, they wrote a letter like this: "Sir, apparently you are running from us and we really don't want you to live this way. Please know that we forgive you and absolve you of all liability. You owe us nothing. My wife and I are both signing this letter so you can live free. We only ask that you let us know you received the letter and that you accept what we say."

There was no answer.

A couple of months later, they sent a copy of the letter. This one came back. Stamped on the front was, "Moved, left no forwarding address." He was running.

My parents renewed the hunt. Another year passed before they found him. He had moved a great distance away. Once again, they wrote him. This time, the letter expressed more urgency.

"Sir, obviously you are running from us and we really, really don't want you to live this way. Please, please know that we forgive you and you owe us nothing. We want you to live free, so my wife and I are signing this letter again. We only ask that you let us know that you received the letter and you accept what we say."

There was no answer.

A couple of months later, they sent a copy of the letter. This one came back stamped on the front, "Moved, left no forwarding address." He was running. Unlike our God who is much more persistent, this attempt ended my parents' search.

So, somewhere on this planet, a man still runs, terrified that I might find him. Yet he holds in his hands a letter, all that he needs to live free. He just doesn't believe it and won't receive it.

As I pondered this event, I realized that millions more on this planet are running from God, terrified that He might find them, yet they hold in their hands a "letter," a Bible–all they need to live free. They just don't believe it and won't receive it.

Discussion:

1. How has God pursued you in the past?
2. Do you know someone who is running? What actions do you observe?
3. Have you ever tried to let someone know that you forgive them? What was the response?

Hands

The Right Hand

Well over a billion people on this planet eat with their hands, not because they don't know better—it is their tradition, a revered and very efficient way of life. One common thread exists for those who eat with their hands: they *all* eat with their *right* hand.

This is more than symbolic, since the left hand is reserved for personal cleanliness functions. In countries where this right hand tradition is strongest, if you touch a dish on the table with your left hand, the dish will be silently and immediately removed. Don't expect your host to correct you. He never will. He may wonder at your rudeness or crudeness, but he will never correct you.

Once, on my first trip to India in 1976, I was eating in the home of an outstanding Christian leader. Their precocious and verbal four-year-old son had been banished to another room to eat while I was there. Part way through the meal, I heard him loudly call for his father's attention. When his father responded, the boy asked, "Is he eating with his left hand?"

Obviously, he had been warned that I might do so and was told not to make an issue of it. To the embarrassed father, I smiled and said, "Well, I know some important things to remember, now."

This hand separation does, as would be expected, extend to symbolism. In Zimbabwe, I carefully gave and received gifts only with my right hand. To do otherwise could be an insult unless the person knew you very well and understood that you were simply an ignorant American.

One significant symbolism parks unforgettably in my mind. Often, when a gift is presented to someone, they will receive the gift with their right hand and will cup their left hand under their right hand as if to give support. This is their way of saying that your gift is too heavy or too much for them to receive only with one hand, so they must support their hand. This is their way of honoring your worthiness or the value of your gift as they also say, "Thank you."

In similar fashion, when you shake hands with someone, he might grasp his right wrist with his left hand as a way of saying that shaking hands with you is too heavy for him, as if to say "I am unworthy to be shaking hands with you." People say many things nonverbally if you carefully observe.

Pocket Hands

Zimbabwean native men do not walk around with their hands in their pockets as I and many Americans nonchalantly do. They keep their hands out of their pockets, because they believe that to put them in your pockets means that you have money or some reason to put your hands there. This makes pocket hands a signal of wealth or position. Being mostly poor people, they consider it arrogant to place their hands in their pockets. Perhaps it is OK for us Americans to walk around with our hands in our pockets, since, by world standards, we are all wealthy, but not them.

I shall never forget a dramatic moment in the history of the Zimbabwean Church. A Bible school had been built and in full swing for several years, but they had no chapel, no gathering place for the students or meeting hall for conferences. With their own hands they dug the foundations, made the bricks and built a large building. I was there on that joyous day when they dedicated the new building, the largest on campus. The building was filled with pastors and leaders from all over the country.

The speaker, a leading businessman, who led the dedication, at the close of his message told the hands-in-the-pocket tradition, then said, "Now we have something. We are rich. I want everyone to walk around here at the front with their hands in their pockets." I plunged my hands in my pockets and joined them proudly strutting around that building and smiling hard enough to hurt my face.

Grandma's Hands

When my grandparents retired and moved from the farm to the city, I did not know of a promise my grandmother had made. For so long, they lived on a farm somewhat remote from church, even more remote when the bridge washed out, which happened often. My grandmother so hungered to go to church that she promised the Lord that if He let them move to the city, she would go to church every day that she could. That promise deeply affected my life–in this way:

My parents moved away from the city while I was in the ninth grade. Wanting to finish that grade in my school, I persuaded everybody to let me live with my grandparents and finish the ninth grade, ignorant of the fact that I would be going to church almost every night.

Whenever revival meetings appeared in the newspaper, we geared up Grandpa and Grandma's old Pontiac and began the search/drive for wherever the meeting would be located. We saw some strange things and some wonderful things.

Since my grandmother drove as one trained on a trafficless farm, my grandfather's blindness worked to his benefit. She felt that proper driving meant positioning the hood ornament over the line in the middle of the road. Grandpa was mercifully blind.

The strangeness of some meetings fueled good discussions when we returned home. Grandpa helped me learn how to pick out the Biblical from the non-Biblical in our observation. I value that more now than I did then.

However, living in their home left me with some warm memories as well as hot knowledge. My grandmother lived in the kitchen. She loved me and I knew it. Whenever I passed nearby in the kitchen, she would reach up and pat me on the cheek. Flour from her hands flew everywhere. If I licked my lips, she baked me a chocolate cake.

They don't make cakes like that any more. Or hands.

Going to church every night had an upside apart from the spiritual. When we arrived home, she always made me a sandwich and a cup of tea. So, anytime I visit you and refuse coffee asking instead for a cup of tea, think of my grandma's hands.

Discussion:

1. What customs in your life involve the use of your hands? What meanings do they have?
2. If someone were to write a story in the future about your hands, what might they say?
3. If you could "wash your hands" of some particular problem, what would it be?

Jake

Jake broke the meter on meanness. He was a logger whose favorite sport, when he had a bit of alcohol in his system, was to go to a little local church and beat up the deacons. Jake's meanness was exceeded only by his ugliness. The one tooth remaining in the front of his mouth deterred any smiles and inhibited anyone seeking a smile.

I met Jake only because of one remarkable event. My father, severely injured in an accident when I was six years old, attempted to return to ministry by teaching for a week at a tiny church in a logging community. Scurrying to find beds for each member of the family, the church assigned me that week to the home of a faithful church-going lady who had a son my age.

The house sat near the top of a wooded hill. Water was retrieved by walking about two hundred yards down a steep side of the hill to a spring and carrying heavy buckets up to the house. The husband of the house was Jake. I was in enemy territory.

The whole family lived in constant terror worrying that they might set Jake off in a furious and violent tirade. We all walked on eggshells. I almost enjoyed going down the hill for water. At least being away from the house offered some relaxation.

One day the chore assigned to my friend and me meant carrying bucket after bucket of water up that hill. I watched as the large black pot of water was heated up by a wood fire outside so clothes could be scrubbed on an old "scrub board" and hung out to dry. Washing was hard work but that was life and no other alternatives presented themselves.

Like yesterday, I can remember the Wednesday night when Jake showed up at church. Nervousness skittered across the crowd. Was Jake drunk? Was he going to beat someone up? Why was Jake even here? He never comes to church except to beat someone up. But this was Jake's night. At the invitation, Jake stood and made his way down front to kneel. Everyone was awestruck. They wondered if this was a new trick of Jake's.

The next night, Jake returned. Shock, like a small earthquake registered on each person. At the midpoint of the service, my father asked if anyone wanted to report on what God was doing in their lives. Jake stood up and said, "I have something to say." I could tell that he would be permitted to say anything he wanted.

"Last night when I came here, I hated you people." Heads nodded in recognition of that fact. "But something happened to me and I don't understand this, but tonight I love you." He smiled and the one ugly tooth had somehow become beautiful. Even at the tender age of six, I knew that Jake had the goods. I saw the fruit in the home where I was staying. Joy reigned. Salvation does that!

Other similar events in my life I decided to call "Jake moments." Sunday morning I had finished a message in a small suburb community church in a rural area of Southern California. The invitation was being issued by the pastor. I sat and watched. Suddenly a man midway back in the congregation slowly stood up. He stood there for just a second and his wife sitting next to him shot up, wrapped her arms around him and began to sob. I knew at that moment that a home had been restored. Joy would now reign. I wept. And remembered Jake.

In the Dakotas, I watched as a high school teenager, newly in the kingdom, was hugged by his father, also new in the kingdom, for the first time in his life. They both were sobbing like babies. Another Jake moment.

Another moment happened in Philadelphia, just like it had happened years earlier in that small South Dakota town. At the close of a men's retreat, I was watching as God "was doing His thing" in the hearts of the men during a communion service, when I spotted a man coming toward me whose feet seemed not to be touching the ground as he bounded along, his face locked in a maximum smile. His story made it clear. "Tonight, my father became a Christian and for the first time, I heard him say 'I love you' to me."

I just put down a letter from a young lady in Washington State thanking me for the fact that her grandfather had accepted the Lord in a service I led. Her grandfather, whom she loved dearly, had resisted following the Lord until that moment and he said that I made it so clear. Now he had passed away and the family was ecstatic that he knew the Lord. Jake, you didn't know what you started.

The sermon had concluded at Ft. Lauderdale. The worship team was playing and Bob Coy, the pastor, had invited those who wanted to become Christians to come forward. I stood slightly to his side and watched. I noticed an old man making his way down toward the front. That is unusual enough to catch my attention.

He wasted no time and, rather than stand waiting for instructions to go to a prayer room, fell to his knees at the steps of the platform. Moved by that, I wondered what was going on in his heart. I should have watched for two hearts. A form moved by me on the platform, almost unnoticed, until he knelt beside the old man. It was George, one of the worship musicians and that was his dad who had come forward. He had prayed for his dad for a long time and now the fruit knelt father and son beside each other. A Jake moment.

Shortly before my 21st birthday, I conducted a week of meetings in my old home church in Chester, Oklahoma, where they were kind enough to give this old homeboy a chance. In that community lived a farmer known for his hostility to

Christianity. His wife was a strong and faithful Christian who loved to be involved in the church but her husband despised every moment.

If he spotted her car on the road, he would jump in his pickup and leave his field to chase her. He would stop and search her car to make sure she wasn't taking food or some other form of gift to the church. But the meaner he got, the nicer she treated him.

I knew him and was most shocked to see him come to one of the evening services. At the close, in response to the invitation, he quickly made his way forward and knelt. I couldn't believe what I was seeing. Afterward, I made a mistake and asked him what I said that had moved him to come forward. He assured me his move had nothing to do with what I said. He only wanted me to hurry up and quit so he could get saved. He told me that he could not continue his way of living. He made life a hell for his wife and the worse he treated her the better she treated him. He decided that he had to have what she had. When I last saw him before he went to be with the Lord, he was a deacon.

Another Jake.

Maybe you have a "Jake" moment in your life.

Maybe you need one.

Discussion:

1. Who experienced the most dramatic conversion you have seen? What was the change?
2. For whom are you praying now for a conversion and what change do you expect to see?
3. From whom would you like to hear "I love you," and to whom would you like to say "I love you"?

Airport Drama

When surrounded by crowds, you rarely notice individuals; however, some personal scenes grab your attention and will not release. Often, as I wait for a plane, I observe personal anguish or tragedies–perhaps people arriving for a funeral or accompanying someone virtually disabled. You try not to stare, but you notice and share in their pain.

I noticed something different happening in Denver. I was waiting for my plane connection to arrive and concentrating on my reading. There are always others waiting to greet arrivals, but this group caught my eye. An older couple, accompanied by a nervously pacing young man, looked out the window by the gate to see if the plane had arrived. The older couple seemed to feel out of place in the airport. Through his thick glasses I could see quizzical and concerned eyes. In the noise, only smatterings of conversation came through.

"Are you sure she is coming?"

"Yes, she said this flight."

"Does she know we want to see her?"

"No."

"Does she want to see us?"

"She doesn't know you are here. This is a surprise."

As the intercom announced that the plane had landed, the younger man quickly ushered the couple across the hall where they would not be readily seen, then he came back to wait beside the door for passengers. Anxious glances passed back and forth across the hall. By now, they had my complete attention though I tried not to be too obvious.

My detective mind started to piece the scene together. Was this a runaway coming home? Was this a long-lost relative being reunited? Was a torn relationship about to be repaired? Was this young chap the engineer?

With the young man, I watched each person burst from the walkway leading from the plane. I tried to guess which one it would be. No one brightened his face–no recognition came. Finally, the exodus stopped; the man's glances and agitation were matched by the couple across the hallway. The young man started down the gangway to see if anyone else was coming. No one was.

The older couple, walking in a pool of disappointment made their way across the aisle to join the young man. All smiles were gone. His best efforts had not produced the healing connection. One more glance down the walkway from the plane proved futile. They turned to go. He shrugged and said, "I don't understand. This is the plane she was supposed to be on. I don't understand." I found my feelings matching theirs.

As they began to walk away, heightened hope would not let the young man go without one more look down the walkway. Aha! Indeed someone was coming. I could see a baby stroller just coming away from the plane. Quiet conversation became shouted orders. The older couple rushed back to their place across the terminal aisle. The man greeted the young lady as she came through the door, then knelt down to see the baby. The conversation began.

"I was worried. The plane emptied and I did not see you." She ignored his statement to place her own question.

"Do you think they want to see me? Are they angry?" Just as he was smiling to answer, the older couple approached. Tears followed the embraces and smiles. As the older couple knelt to touch the baby, the girl said to the child, "Meet your grandpa and grandma." Reunion complete. Happiness restored. Prodigal returned. Now I understood.

As they walked away, I raised my paper higher and closer to my face. I'm still not comfortable letting people watch me cry.

Discussion:

1. What kind of scene makes you cry?
2. Did you ever "come home" or know someone who did? What was the reception like?
3. How did individuals in this story act like God?

Kenneth

In research for a possible history book, I discovered that Kenneth was just days away from election as state leader in his denomination. Then he was struck down. I also discovered that state leaders in that denomination had a horrible record in preserving their children from the disillusionment of the politics of that office.

What might have happened to me, his son, had he received that office? I don't know. Some understandings await their fulfillment in Heaven. Others also wondered at his accident that left his left side paralyzed and downgraded him from leader to survivor (see *The Runner*). However, his spirit was never broken (see *Half A Brain* and *Jake*).

This reduction from being the breadwinner of the household never sat well with him. Every few months birthed a new attempt to live gainfully. He raised hogs, raised rabbits, trapped wild rabbits, hauled wheat. I say *he* but I really mean *we*. Everywhere he went, I had to go as his caretaker and do most of the work. I was killing and skinning rabbits at age eight, gathering slop (That is a lost word in our urban society.) for hogs by age nine. This whole intrusion into my childhood was a slingshot to maturity.

His loss of earning power also meant poverty for the family and living in conditions that news programs, a decade later, were spotlighting.

Though this grinds on the core of any man, it failed to break his spirit. Also, never once did he seek or receive any form of government assistance to alleviate our need.

If you were to describe my Dad by one word, it would be *believer*. He trusted God. Whatever else you might say to describe him, you had to say "He trusted God." His Bible, which I now own, is frayed from constant use. Every trip home from college included a time for us to discuss the Bible together. Often, we would have to go over passages again and again, because he kept forgetting what we had discussed. Now I can see how God was making sure that I learned.

Actually, our real learning came from the Bible. Before I began my brief career as a newsboy, Dad took me to Proverbs and had me read 22:1, "A good name is rather to be chosen than great riches and loving favor rather than silver and gold." Whatever my business in life might be, uprightness far exceeded wealth in desirability.

The night before I left for college, he stood at my bedroom door while I slept (as he related to me later) and prayed for me. Then he said, "Well, Gayle, I have taken you as far as I can. From now on it is just you and God." I cannot even write this without crying.

He (we) depended upon the miraculous. Survival was impossible without God's intervention, but intervene God did! By the time I headed for college, the reality of God and His Word were so wrapped at the core of me that all attempts by the school's liberal religious approach to weaken or deprive my faith were far too late and much too weak. I, too, had become a *believer*.

His injuries took their final toll after thirty-two years, but the memory of his greatness and his wealth of friends filled the church which he had founded and built and where his funeral service was conducted. At his funeral my two brothers and I stood in front of his casket and made the following statement to all those who had gathered:

"Our father did not leave a financial empire for us to carry on. Many things that a dad normally does with his sons, ours was unable to do. He was unable to teach us many things that a dad normally teaches. But he did leave us something that he had. He left us with a love of God, a love for the Bible, a love of people, an understanding of worship and an inability to hate. We feel that he has left us only those things that will last. So we stand before you as his sons and declare publicly that we will follow his God."

Discussion:

1. Describe the joys and difficulties of relating to your father.
2. How has being a follower of Jesus affected your relationship with your father?
3. If you are a father, what do you wish most for your children or your family?

JCC VP

I was downtown to deliver the high school paper to the local newspaper who would carry it as a whole page in their Friday edition. From an office across the street, a businessman beckoned for me to come over. He was the vice president of the National Junior Chamber of Commerce and I was honored that he noticed me, a mere high school student.

I sat down in his office wondering why he flagged me. He said that he had been watching my activities in high school and wanted to compliment me. He also wanted to contribute something to my life, so he began a short lecture on what he considered to be the three most important decisions a person would ever make.

"The most important," he said, "is the decision about whom you will serve. I want to urge you to truly serve God." That decision, I knew, I had already made.

"Second, you must decide what you will do with your life, how you will make a living, what contribution you will make to society." I thought I had that settled in a desire to be a medical doctor.

"Finally, you must decide who your partner will be in life. Failure to make wise decisions in any of these three can destroy you." This decision was yet to be made in my life.

I thanked him and left, pondering this moment, the only time, as it turned out, that I would ever meet him, but, nonetheless, a moment filled with wisdom.

Discussion:

1. When you need advice, where do you go?
2. What is the best advice you ever received?
3. Which of the three decisions in our story have you made? Describe how and when you did.

Charlie Brown

He refused to tell me later what he thought of me the first time we met. I remember that meeting well. My relationship with his daughter had grown to the point that it was time for me to meet her parents. Trailways bus was the only way to get to Ripley. Well, one could drive if one possessed a car, but I was a poverty-struck college freshman who had hitchhiked from Jackson, Mississippi to Memphis, Tennessee as my monthly custom had become.

The bus inched for twenty years, or so it seemed to my sweaty palms as we headed north. Three earthquakes rumbled through my heart. Earthquake number one was akin to stag fever, that "awe" that disables the trigger finger when prey is spotted. So with me. I was trying to be super cool so that Tennessee's best doe, which I had cornered in the bus, wouldn't be skittish and run.

Earthquake two shook my most vulnerable pillars. I was a bull being run into the auctioneer's arena to see if anyone would buy. This was an "approval" run. Would they like me or wouldn't they? That question shatters an eighteen-year-old far more than a mid-century man.

Strike three (I mean earthquake three.) was an embarrassing physical condition caused by an activity that has since been declared illegal. Upperclassmen at the college I had just entered hazed the freshmen by shaving their heads when they arrived and forcing them to wear little skull-cap beanies. So, I was totally bald, and bald was not *in* for eighteen-year-olds in 1956.

I still don't think my head is designed for bald though nature seems to have now bettered me in that argument. Indeed, I haven't any indication that nature was even listening to me. Football practice and a training table had reduced my neck and increased my shoulders. Tables, reductions and increases still go on, but the locations are different. I looked like a stump with a bowling ball sitting on top! I can laugh about it now.

Fortunately, my doe's family was too civil to laugh in my presence. I'm not sure they ever laughed–maybe prayed, cried, took aspirin, but not laughed.

It must have been stressful for him, because years later when I asked him what he thought when he first met me, he would only say, "We love you, son."

"I know that, Dad, but what did you first think of me?"

"It's OK. We love you, son!"

That was all I could get out of him. And he did love me, too. Every meal, he would hover over me making sure my plate was always full long after I was–urging me like some protective mother every minute on the minute to eat–keeping my hands busier refusing than forking.

He was thoroughly Christian. I watched him prove that with his life. The most agitated I ever saw him resulted from a misunderstanding with a neighbor. He could not rest until the problem had been resolved. He didn't bother to read the paper or listen to the news much, so his mind lacked the clutter of our day. He lived by priceless values ignored by those who strive for gold. He loved God and people and sought to provide all things honest in the eyes of man.

Newspapers were ignorant of his name, but the townspeople weren't. They held him in highest respect. If he said something, it was true. If he recommended, they seriously considered. As a twenty-one-year-old looking for places to preach, he took me to meet three people, mildly suggested they ought to have me preach for them and I had three meetings scheduled immediately.

I married his daughter on Thanksgiving Day of 1957. Only hospitals and police stations even thought of being open on that day in this country town, but my car had rejected its muffler that morning, emitting a sound hardly appropriate to ferry my bride and his last child away from him. No problem. He made two phone calls and a store plus a service station opened to supply and install a muffler on the car on this holiday. Everyone seemed happy to accommodate him.

On one of my last visits with him, I noticed a plaque on the wall that I had not seen there before. His church presented a certificate to him to acknowledge and honor his fifty years as a deacon. A doctorate from Harvard could not have been a higher honor.

Once, he grabbed my heart in a way that I was never able to tell him. I had been preaching in

Nashville and had some spare time, so I rented a car and drove over to visit with them. Exhausted, I took time for a nap and asked them to awaken me for dinner. When the time came, Dad entered the room, crawled onto the bed and kissed me on the cheek. "It's time to get up, son."

The severe circumstances of my own childhood had left an empty spot where tendernesses like that are supposed to lodge. At that moment, Dad Brown had loosened that crusty lid and poured a fresh emotional freedom into my jar. It was too deep for me to ever tell him.

I miss him. He went to be with the Lord in 1987. He was eighty-seven. Charlie Brown of Ripley, Tennessee. Dad Brown. My father-in-law.

Discussion:

1. If you are an "in-law," what could cause your new relatives to pick you as a friend if you were not in the family?
2. In what ways have you grown because of in-laws? This can include overcoming difficulties.
3. What anxieties have you faced in choosing a spouse for life?

Elma

Elma was the strong one. A middle daughter in a family of nine brothers and an older sister, responsibility fell to her in that early 1900's family that would have staggered a lesser person. Elma was very young when she and Charlie finally eloped (after several unsuccessful attempts) and let a Justice of the Peace tie the knot. He tied it well.

When I met Elma, she and Charlie ran a "mom and pop" grocery store (an institution now almost extinct) beside the highway next to their house. Her quiet strength became quickly obvious. She was now caring for her own mother who lived out her declining years in a cabin behind their house.

Though she would laugh a lot, especially if I said something funny, she was mostly matter-of-fact. Being an entrepreneur, wife, mother and nurse meant there was too much to do to take time for small talk. She watched me carefully, wondering at this shaved-head, beaten-faced, college freshman football player who had come to ask if they would turn their only cherished daughter over to him to take her away forever.

It was a difficult year waiting for the strange, shaved-head outsider to take away her daughter. Ensuing hairier visits did little to ease her misgivings.

There were certain "givens" in her life:
She never missed church.
She never considered sin.
She never let an enemy remain one.
She never complained.

She never considered hospitality anything but natural. Her home was constant host to family who often lived with her for extended periods, to large meals, to other guests.

The tragedy of losing the youngest of three sons in a drowning accident hung constantly, unspoken in her heart. Her parenting heart was bigger than the four children naturally allotted to her, so she frequently kept foster children.

She celebrated sixty years of faithfulness with Charlie and could have celebrated more had it not been for the illness that ended his life.

As she waits out her own days in a care center visited daily by her children, but largely unaware of her surroundings, it seems further evidence that a just God would arrange for a resurrection.

Discussion:

1. What work or chores do you have simply because you are in a family?
2. What work do you do that is not required of you, simply because you have the skills and enjoy doing it?
3. What would you say you have been doing for the "long haul?"

Ada

When I was in high school in Greenwood, Mississippi, a national Junior Chamber of Commerce leader asked me to drop by his office. He had something he wanted to say to me. In summary, he said, "Every person makes three great choices: whom he will serve, what he will do and with whom he will spend his life. Be wise in those choices." (see *JCC VP*)

The choice of whom I would serve had long been settled. I never wanted to be anything but a follower of Jesus. I thought I had settled the second–to be a surgeon. The third was still ahead of me. I didn't know that all would be settled within a year and in surprising ways.

In February of 1956, I was featured in a national youth magazine because of some honors that had come to me in high school. A young lady who subscribed to the magazine and lived about two hundred miles away saw the article and did a most uncharacteristic thing for her–she wrote me a letter suggesting that we exchange ideas about youth work since we were both involved in church leadership.

Her neat, left-slanted handwriting that carefully detailed her faith captured my interest. I was encouraged by the fact that, because of her faithful Christian service, the same youth magazine that featured me gave a similar write-up of her.

More letters and ideas and then photos were exchanged between Ripley, Tennessee and Greenwood until she moved to Memphis to continue schooling and told me to come see her if I was ever up that way.

I happened to be "ever up that way" one day and met Ada Faye Brown one summer afternoon in 1956. She was quite popular, being courted by an extensive group of men, but I soon had her exclusive attention. Now that I had a reason to go to Memphis, I would catch a ride with whomever I could.

College moved me one hundred miles farther away, but about once a month as a shaved-head freshman football player, I would thumb a ride up Highway 51 from Jackson, Mississippi to Memphis. There I stayed in the YMCA, ready to see Ada every chance her job would permit on a weekend, then take a miserable 1:00 a.m. bus ride back to Jackson.

A kickoff collision at a football game in Arkansas cracked my back in four places and I was flown back to Jackson for a week's stay in the hospital. By the middle of the week, Ada was there to see me and that was all I needed to make my decision.

Thanksgiving Day was bitterly cold in Memphis and the brace I wore under my shirt seemed to make me more vulnerable to the wind, but all that was inconsequential to the "yes" I had received from her that day. A year later, also on Thanksgiving Day, my father tied the knot for us in her home church in Ripley.

Now, all the great decisions had been made and I was only nineteen. God had tugged me toward preaching and delivered Tennessee's best to me.

I have often kidded Ada that she agreed to marry a future surgeon but ended up with a poor preacher. She assured me that she knew all along she would marry a preacher. I believe that, too. Her teen years were filled with traveling and playing the piano for church functions.

Her life had been as resolved as my own. She wanted only to be a follower of Jesus. Her family was deeply involved with the church–her father a fifty-year veteran of deaconship.

Nonetheless, one is never quite prepared for the road marriage takes. Despite what all the manuals say, the constantly new adventure of marriage is similar to walking on water. Ada lived on the water.

She has borne the pain of four births and one miscarriage and loved our children to successful adulthood. She mastered both the kitchen and the checkbook, carefully stewarding us to far more than my salary should ever provide. Her hospitality, often instant and sometimes massive, was a model others have copied. The "early junkyard" sow's-ear-of-provision I gave her was woven into a silk purse of decorative skill making our home a center of comfort.

Never once could I wonder about her faithfulness though she was often alone from my extensive travels. We have laughed, we have played, we have loved and we have fought. On my schedule for late November every year, a large block of time is marked "celebration." During that time, thanks to airlines who have seen my face frequently enough to reward me, Ada and I will be in *Who Knows Where* celebrating umpteen years of marriage—a tribute to a lady who had the character to make marriage happen.

"Thanksgiving" seems an appropriate name for *our* day.

Discussion:

1. If you are married, tell how you and your spouse met. What were some of the memorable marks of your courtship?
2. What role do you feel God has played in the strong relationships you have developed.
3. What main strengths do you feel your spouse or a close friend has?

Half a Brain

My Friend

My friend Denny called me often to his office to share valuable insights he had learned from the Bible and, knowing my penchant for story telling, the latest parables or stories he thought I might use. I grew to appreciate him very much. In one of those tragedies I will not understand until I get to Heaven, Denny had a heart attack as a very young man, apparently a genetic anomaly. Unfortunately, the medical people arrived in time to save his life, but not in time to save his brain.

Now, he was reduced to a six-year-old in mentality. Though married, he did not understand what that meant. He spoke and thought as a child. That is, until you got him into church. Whenever he was brought to church, as the songs were being sung, he sang as if normal. When the Scripture was being quoted, his lips would move in remembrance. Something deeper than the damaged brain existed inside him, something that the damage could not touch, something written far deeper than simple memory.

My Mother-in-law

My mother-in-law has lived to a great age and lived profitably. She resisted the prospect of being out of her home and in some sort of institutional care system. However, as Alzheimers disease reduced her ability to care for herself, a serious hospital stay proved the successful bridge. By this time, most of her conversation was incoherent or wildly inappropriate. Except for one thing which my wife reported to me after a stay with her.

Whenever she prayed, her mind and her words were totally coherent and logical. As she lay helpless in the hospital bed, her spirit was not helpless. For long periods of time, she would march through her relatives' names praying for them, relate the need of her church in prayer, pray for people she didn't even know. Somehow, beneath all the brain cells affected by the disease, there lay a fully alert ability to communicate with her God. As long as she was talking to Him, she was totally coherent.

My Father

My father was severely injured in an airplane accident as a young man and he was left disabled with a damaged brain and a paralyzed left side. Throughout his now-diminished life, he continued unswervingly to serve the Lord. Though livelihood now came from menial jobs rather than pastoring as in the past, his life of Bible study and worship and integrity never varied. Both my parents stood as giant examples for me to follow.

When my father died at age sixty-five, an autopsy revealed that half of his brain was dead. For thirty-two years he had lived for God with half of his brain dead!

You can serve God with half a brain!
There's hope for all of us!

After publishing these stories in my newsletter called *Servant Quarters*, I received the following letter in response. It is a classic.

Dear Gayle,

About your recent article *Half A Brain*. This is one of those notes where you want to be as visual and graphic as possible and know you'll fall short.

My husband is brain damaged (one of the early drug rebels of the 60's–70's). By God's limitless grace, I know who he is inside and through much pain and growth over twenty years, it is enough. We are at great peace in our marriage and have a fine godly son.

But it's times like this morning, when I read him the article, that (although he has no voice nor initiative to initiate any act) he is a responder. And if only you could have heard his response to that blessed article! A voice of laughter came through as he chuckled in agreement with every word! Again, remember, he has no voice!

So, it was miraculous in that sense and held so much joy that it needed to be shared.

Nancy
California

Discussion:

1. Describe someone you know who serves the Lord in spite of great disability.
2. What could shake your faith if it happened to you?
3. What measures are you taking to fill your spirit with good things?

Johnny Abide

My sophomore year in high school had more than its share of misery. In the ninth grade, I had begun to play football and was first-team fullback. Discount the fact that we lost all of our games. Then my family moved to a southern state and a city who viewed high school football as semi-pro. Football took on a new meaning to me.

In fact, the level of play in this new school was so high that they had eighty people who went out for football and only seventy-nine uniforms. I did not dress out.

I wasn't about to go to the games and have people ask me, "Aren't you supposed to be out there playing?" You can say you are hurt only for so long a time. (Well, my feelings were hurt!) So, in the absence of dressing for the games, I got involved in a series of church activities on Friday nights that grew in their success and effectiveness. The last game of the season coincided with a major church youth activity we had planned. Then the bottom dropped out of my world.

Several players had been injured and some had dropped out, so uniforms were now available for that last game. The coach said to me, "Gayle I want you to dress out for this last game."

"Aw, Coach, I haven't been dressing out all season and I have become involved in some church activities. This Friday is our big night."

"Gayle, if you ever want to play on this team or be anything at this school, you will dress out this Friday night."

"But, Coach, I am in charge and I have to be at the meeting."

"Gayle, you can get someone else to be in charge. You dress out!"

I walked in misery after that. There was no one else who could handle the responsibility. Each day brought me closer to that fateful decision. Inside, I shriveled noticeably. I wanted to be on the team. I wanted to be involved in school activities, and I also knew that football and the coach had the power to destroy my future.

Friday arrived, the teachers always let us football players out early on Friday, and I managed to take advantage of that perk whether I dressed out or not. No joy accompanied the early release on that day. The decision could be delayed no longer.

I leaned against my hallway locker looking out on what I thought would be my last happy day. Suddenly, bounding up the stairway beside me came Johnny Abide. I didn't want to see Johnny. He was the football star. Every week, his name filled the sports page: "Johnny Abide scores 300 points. Johnny Abide runs 700-yard touchdown." He was the last person I wanted to see. I could not escape.

"Gayle, what's wrong with you. You look like your world has caved in. What is going on?"

I decided to tell him. "Johnny, you know that I have not been dressing out this season for the games. So, I have become very involved in some church activities that take place on Friday nights. Tonight is our big event, but the coach has told me I have to dress out now that some uniforms are available. I don't know what to do."

"Gayle, I don't believe this. If you dress out tonight, I will personally beat you up!"

My decision was getting clearer.

"I'm a football star (I knew that.) and my picture is in the paper every week, but after I leave this school they will forget about me and all that stuff will not help me one bit. What you are doing is eternal and doesn't even compare with this stupid game. If you are willing to give up something that worthwhile just to dress out for one game, you are not as smart as I thought you were. I will personally beat you up."

My decision was made. I did not know that Johnny was a Christian. He moved in different circles than I. My heart was free. The coach never noticed that I wasn't there. I made the first team the next two seasons. At the end of my high school days, the coach wrote a letter of recommendation for me that stated that he hoped his two sons would turn out just like me.

Yet I came so close to ditching my responsibilities for such worthless reasons. I don't like getting beat up. I guess the Lord knew that.

Discussion:

1. Describe some major decisions you have made in your life. Did anyone help you make them?
2. When have you been surprised at how well things turned out for you after you made a right but difficult choice?
3. In what areas do you not see clearly and how do you seek help in those areas?

Eugene

Puberty clobbered me terminally about age thirteen. Life and decisions and feelings tugged relentlessly and pulled me along in its turbulent cloud of dust. I needed help. Enter, Eugene.

Eugene, my junior high school Sunday School teacher, sensed my need and moved gently into my life. No patronizing "Be at ease, kid, I am here." Instead, he made me feel that the finest thing that could happen to him would be for me to spend time with him on Saturdays. I was willing to "bless" him.

We attended baseball games, played miniature golf, drank root beer and talked...and talked...and talked. I found myself wanting to serve God like Eugene. Perhaps you would never know him if I didn't tell this story. Not much recommended him to the world. He had no high-paying job, or big house, or social position, or memorable looks. He was simply a servant, sensitive to those young people who might need help. He was an excellent violin player, but received few accolades in the church world. Nonetheless, he had touched me significantly during a most needy time of my life.

When I left that city at the end of my junior high days, I did not thank him for what he had done for me. Junior highers do not know that word. I did not write to him. Junior highers are illiterate. As far as he knew, I dropped off the surface of the earth. I knew nothing more of him, except his signature on my soul.

Sixteen years later, now on the headquarters staff of a denomination, I sat in my corner office, doing what editors do, when I heard his voice: "Is this where you subscribe to *Youth Alive*?" Memories flooded me as I jumped up and ran to the front.

"Eugene!"

He looked at me for a few seconds and responded, "Are you Gayle Erwin?"

"Yes."

"What are you doing here?" (He probably thought I was in prison by now.)

"You don't know?"

"No. My daughter has come here to nursing school and I want to subscribe to this magazine for her. It is the best thing I have ever seen."

"You don't know that I created it and edit it?"

"No! You are kidding!"

"Eugene, this is just the bread you cast on the water coming home to you. You blessed me when I was a teenager and now I get to bless your daughter. This is what happens in the Kingdom of God."

We reminisced for a while and then parted. I didn't know if I would ever see him again, but one day he called and said he was coming to see his daughter in school and accepted my invitation to stay at our house. That night, my wife suffered a painful miscarriage. Once again, I found Eugene ministering to us at a time of need.

I developed a close friendship with the state youth leader where Eugene lived. During one of our talk times, we discovered that we both attended the same church during junior high days. "Why didn't I know you then?" I asked.

"Because you are two years older than I am and wouldn't give me the time of day."

"Oh." Then I remembered, "There was a teacher in that church who deeply touched my life."

Before I could say another word, he blurted out, "It was Eugene, wasn't it."

"Yes."

"Me, too. You see, I am an orphan and I really needed help at that age. Eugene seemed to sense that and just moved into my life...."

We marveled at God's faithfulness to us and thanked Him for sending Eugene. Eugene moved (I didn't know that.) and I moved (He didn't know that.) and once again we dropped off each other's radar screen. I was to have two more significant meetings with him, however, one was not face-to-face.

When I first flew to California to prepare to move, I rose early, bought an Orange County newspaper to look for a house to rent. Since I am a newshound, I took my time getting to the classifieds. On page 2, a small paragraph item caught my eye. The city water utility of an Oklahoma town had just received a check from Eugene years after he had moved away with a letter of apology. He stated that the bill was lost in the move and now that he had found it, as a Christian, he must pay the full amount with interest. So rare an ethic had made it all the way to a California newspaper.

Twenty more years passed without seeing him until one day he found out that I was coming to Dallas to teach at a church. He made his way there that morning to hear me speak to an audience for the first time...ever. When I stood to speak and saw him sitting on the back pew, I paused and informed the congregation that a person who had helped shape my life as a teenager was present and I wanted them to hear his story. I briefly condensed the story of the effect Eugene had on me and expressed my gratitude to him.

I looked back at him, and shouldn't have. He was crying.

Discussion:

1. Name two people other than your parents who have influenced your life and tell how they did.
2. What teacher in school (of any type) has been the most effective for you?
3. Whom did you last call or write and say "Thank you"?

Agnes

Some people apparently get their training in the fire, the Kingdom of God school of survival. This is about just such a person, a lady.

Her father was hostile to the Kingdom and would gladly have stolen her faith. However, as a teenage girl, her direction was chosen. Nothing turned her to the side, although, God knows, all Hell would try.

Agnes' commitment to God took her to a small Bible school far from her home. A revival was flourishing and she had identified with a young denomination. Agnes Pauline Mayo traveled the formidable distance from Mississippi to the farm and oil town of Enid, Oklahoma to what was then known as Southwestern Bible School.

She was pulled swiftly into the fast lane of life at the school. There, she met an energetic young man straight off the farm, a go-getter headed for the top. She married this man named Kenneth. Eighteen months later a son was added to their union.

This son would try her and put her through the first survival wringer as a mother. He was born ugly and large-nosed. At three months of age he gave up naps preferring to demand the constant attention of all persons whether awake or not. At this time, she determined that he would be an only child.

Not only did she have to nurture this child, whose grandparents had called him in a not-too-complimentary way "Meddlesome Mattie," but much of the early child-rearing occurred without a home. The traveling lifestyle of her preacher husband placed her constantly in the homes of others. Not an easy task when you are breastfeeding a hurricane (or at least a strong *gale*).

Life was filled with embarrassing moments. Many complained that she did not discipline the little beast often enough. Others thought that maybe the spankings were why he was so bad. Watching him drag wet newspapers into a church meeting while wearing a mud-caked white suit caused many to doubt her child-rearing abilities. Twenty years later, people would step back in wonder when meeting that child again–in wonder that he was still alive and not in prison.

Destiny in a Small Plane

The desire to introduce people to Jesus led them to a booming war-industry town on the coast of Mississippi to begin a new church. The task would not be easy. Living in the curtained-off corner of a dirt-floored wooden "tabernacle" was hardly the dream of a bride, but it was for the Lord and that was enough.

When they did get a small house, the little beast (whom they had the courage and audacity to name "Gayle") attempted to burn it down. She was forced to learn to jog long before the world would join the craze. Many hours were lost as workers on the new church being built next door would stop to watch as she, with switch in hand, chased the beast around the house shouting threats of ultimate destruction if he didn't stop and get his whipping.

A second son was born who further tested her patience. This new son quickly used his newfound ability of walking to do just that. Police and radio listeners were frequently called to help find the explorer. He also disliked clothing and would dispense with it in church as soon as she turned her back.

There was still never a home, a nest where she could rest as she raised the children. Once the new church building was completed enough to occupy, the back of the basement became living quarters. A water hose hanging over a sheet of plywood became the outside shower that you dared to use only at night.

In that basement home the news came that would permanently change her life and extract more from her than she ever thought she could give–the trial that would move her to greatness. Word came that her husband had been injured in an airplane accident.

Now, she was a poverty-stricken mother, wife, nurse and breadwinner. Now, a home broken in body moved from basement to farm to trailer to shack to house to low-paying job to less-paying job. A world now rested on her shoulders.

The Broken Healthy Home

One thing kept her going. She was in the service of God. Whatever the price or difficulty, it faded compared to the reward she knew God had waiting. Indeed, what the world would have called a dysfunctional family was instead a stable, God-fearing home. How could that be? The answer was simple.

My mother was a saint first and mother second. The things that were supposed to happen in church happened in our home. Prayer, songs, Bible study and faith were not reserved for the pew, but occurred at the breakfast table, the couch, the bedside. Testimony to this fact is that her sons all follow the Lord.

The school of testing was unrelenting. Sometimes, when it seemed that every miracle would wait until the last minute before happening, I could hear her crying and praying as she asked the Lord how long this would continue. A third son came along and she had to feed five stomachs.

I would like to say that life became easy and wealth flowed her way, but I can't. None of her sons became president nor rich, yet the family never dipped into the pockets of the welfare system. The budding brain surgeon who was her first son merely became another preacher and the best he (the little beast named Gayle) can do for her is write this tribute and help fulfill her desire to introduce people to Jesus.

But one thing overrides all else. Her life was lived unquestioningly for the Lord. Agnes Pauline Mayo Erwin was thoroughly saved!

After thirty-two years of caring for an invalid husband, death separated them. That had been her vow forty years earlier—*'til death do us part*. She kept her promise.

God had joys still waiting for her. Another man (Raymond) came into her life and she became Agnes Pauline Mayo Erwin Bazer. We still call her "Mom" for short, probably should call her "St. Mom." Her new husband, a saint himself, is restoring what the cankerworm had eaten.

In November of 1992, she celebrated seventy-five years. Saint Mom! During that November, one of the churches she helped found honored her work. Along with them, we, Gayle Dean, Jesse Matthew and Kenneth Wayne, her sons, rose up and called her blessed.

Discussion:

1. What is the "Mother's Day" ritual at your house? If your mother isn't living, what were the rituals that you remember?
2. What kinds of pain and heartache did you bring to your mother? How have you tried to heal that?
3. What are the greatest joys you have when you are around your mother or you think of her?

Welcome, Now Leave

Our sojourn in that city began in a most un-usual manner. The decision had been made to return from living in Oklahoma City to start a new church. The house formerly lived in by a city official was available. My parents purchased it. The neighborhood knew that building plans were being made for the adjacent vacant lot. This was not to the neighborhood's liking.

When we arrived with our furniture, we were met at the door by a representative of the neighborhood with a petition signed by everyone (except one person) within a three-block radius informing us that we were not welcome and all legal efforts would be made to block our activities. They felt that we would lower the value of their property and they did not want another church.

For months, no one would speak to us. Our neighbor behind us, a policeman and ringleader of the petition effort, would throw his garbage over the fence onto our property. He poisoned our dog, Buster. He had two large, aggressive dogs that he sent out to attack my father when he was out for a walk.

Since my father's left side was paralyzed, he could not run; and as he tried to escape, the dogs chewed up his left hand that hung limp from his disabled shoulder. This policeman appears again at the end of the story.

We cleaned up the house and the adjacent lot and carted away loads of empty liquor bottles in the garage and on the grounds. The fears of the neighborhood were obviously unfounded. One by one, beginning with our next-door neighbors, and often with tears, the people of the neighborhood came and asked forgiveness and asked to personally scratch their names off the petition. When the process was over, only one person's name remained on the petition–the policeman in the house behind us. His signature remains on the petition to this day, but let us come back to him later.

I became immediately active in the high school and began to be known in the city. Every week, my name would be in the city newspaper for some school or community activity. I was on the football team and captain of the debate team.

By the end of my junior year, my activities had enlarged to being president of several school organizations, state president of the Hi-Y and finally president of the student body. Between junior and senior years, I was chosen to be one of the representatives of the city to the Boys' State program. One of the graduating senior leaders strongly urged me to run for governor of Boys' State. I reluctantly agreed to do so and was, indeed, elected to that position as well as sent to Boys' Nation in Washington, D.C.

Being governor of Boys' State was a high honor for that town and when I returned from the state capitol, a crowd had gathered at the steps of the city hall where the American Legion, who sponsored the activity, waited to honor me and my parents. At the city limits, a police motorcade awaited to lead the car I was in, with sirens screaming, to the city hall. Yes (You are ahead of me.), leading the way on his motorcycle was the policeman who lived behind me.

In the book of Esther, Haman built a noose to hang Mordacai, Esther's uncle, but found the rope around his own neck, instead.

Haman rides again!

Discussion:

1. Have you ever been persecuted because you were a Christian and how did it happen?
2. What ways have you seen someone try to destroy a person and instead get destroyed himself? Hint: Look at politics.
3. Have you ever tried to simply do something good and had people misunderstand? Tell about your experience. Did their misunderstanding stop you?

Great Launch

My wife and I made a sentimental journey to the city of my undergraduate college. Warm memories surround the Griffiths, the Lovetts, the Sanders, the Sconiers and others in that city. None of these families permitted me to spend a weekend in the dormitory of the college. If I were sick, it must be at their house, not in the dormitory room. To honor them I named my son Clyde from a representative name of that group of men.

Ada and I married while I was in college and ferried ourselves around in a car that needed towing more than driving (see *The Fleece*). We traded it for one barely better, but at least our feet didn't go through the floorboard. That second car triggered an event I shall never forget.

I was part of the jail ministry sponsored by the Salvation Army but peopled by these men, truck-drivers all, who surrounded me. One Sunday morning, as we descended from the upper floor of the jail in the two-person elevator, Clyde called me aside and said, "Gayle, your car is not going to make it. When you graduate and leave to begin preaching, why not take my new foreign car (Foreign cars were novelties then and this one was as precious as a child to him.) and drive it until you can afford a car of your own?" I was overwhelmed and told him I would consider his generous offer.

He had just finished when J. C. called me aside and said, "Gayle, your car is not going to make it. Why don't you take my car and use it until you can get your own? My wife and I never drive our car because of the company truck I have."

I believed them about my car but hesitated to accept such a large gift from either of them. I didn't know what to do. I planned to take my wife and our daughter Gloria across country preaching as soon as I was graduated. I decided to attempt to purchase a new car.

Much to my amazement, I was able to buy a compact car in the second year they were out though I told the credit manager I did not have a job, had no money except the $100 I paid down, had no promise of a job and had no idea how much I would be making, if any. Why they gave me the loan still causes me to think a miracle occurred.

On this sentimental journey, we visited Charles and Myrtis, people we hold in highest respect and for good reason. On the night of my graduation and before the morning we were to leave on our mission of message, they had insisted that we come to their house. Around coffee and pie, Charles said, "All I own belongs to you. Don't ever let your family go hungry or be deprived as long as I have anything, because it is yours as much as mine."

We left that city with warm and reeling hearts. I knew that God brought me to that city, not to attend a world-class college, but to teach me what love in the Body of Christ actually meant.

Discussion:

1. Who helped you "get a start" in life and what did they do?
2. When you need to "fall back" on someone, who is it?
3. In what ways are you trying to help someone achieve their goals in life?

The Day I Turned Professional

Mrs. Craig, my first grade Sunday School teacher held a special place in my heart. I can still see and hear her playing her mandolin teaching us songs in the little country church in Northwest Oklahoma near Chester. (See if you can find it on your map.) Occasionally they would invite me to spend Sunday afternoon or a few days at their house. One of those pleasant times overlapped with the Fourth of July. I was seven years old.

Chester (Have you found it, yet?), though a small crossroad village, was a major holiday gathering place for the surrounding farming and ranching community. On the Fourth, they would gather to dance, play baseball (what else?) and have turtle races (dry-land terrapins, actually). It was a whole-family event that also included races for the children.

I had never been in a real foot race before and really did not want to risk the embarrassment of a loss to these unknown kids. I entered the race only because the moderator was aggressive in getting us together. Then, suddenly, one small event changed the whole scene.

The leader lined us seven-year-olds up then pulled a big bag full of change (I really don't intend this to be a pun.) out of a sack and announced that a handful of this would go to the winner. I don't know how to describe what happened. It is hard to be philosophical about the emotions of one so young.

Desperation did not drive me, nor resignation, nor ego. Greed! Simply greed! At any rate, I won by several bellies, going away. I think I remember a gasp from the spectators. They knew they were seeing a world-class performance. Only one problem remained. Everyone knew everyone at this gathering, but no one knew me. There was some hesitancy at turning this money over to a complete stranger, and I watched as the call went out for someone to identify me.

I told them I was staying with the Craigs who, unfortunately, were not around at the moment. Finally, reluctantly, they turned the $1.65 over to me and I held in my hand what was, to me, a year's salary.

Now, I hope this revelation of my turning professional will not cause my high school or college to be forced to forfeit any games. I won't worry about junior high school. We lost all six football games anyway.

Discussion:

1. What trophies do you have of your past achievement?
2. When and how did you discover some of your main capabilities?
3. Did you have a childhood adult friend who treated you with special love? Describe them.

Call Me Mister

Dr. Bill MacGowan and his wife, Rene, welcomed me into their home on my first trip to Umtali on the Mozambique border of what was then called Rhodesia in Southern Africa. As an orthopedic surgeon, the raging civil war kept Bill busy and they were somewhat surprised that I had risked sniper fire along the 120-mile stretch of highway between Salisbury (now Harare) and Umtali (now Mutare) to speak in their town.

I tried to think of some way to appear brave, but finally admitted that I was unaware of the road danger until, along the way, my driver asked if I minded that he was armed. Only later did I discover that I was asked to go to Umtali because the other speakers at a conference that brought me to the country refused to go.

Their beautiful home backed against a game reserve, and Bill was once, as he lounged by his pool, temporarily and painfully blinded by a spitting cobra that wandered onto his property. Living in this Garden of Eden land produced a few items to keep you alert.

Bill, a quiet, thoughtful, sometimes-morose person, and I developed a special relationship. Each year, when I would go to their country, now called Zimbabwe, I would stay at least a few nights with them, and, at some point, would bait Bill and purposely draw him into a medical and ethical argument with a broadside against the medical profession.

We kept at it for hours–back and forth through the house, at the table, in the pool. He would lose his cool by splashing water on me, or temporarily stomping off, or threatening to rearrange my body parts if he ever had to operate on me. I thought I was merely having fun, until, one day when he had gone to another part of the house, Rene thanked me.

She said, "The only time Bill ever brightens up, with the war and everything going on, is when you come and bait him, and I really appreciate your bringing him out." I promised to keep a good fight plan for his sake.

A renewal experience made Bill's commitment to God run deep and he sought ways to quietly serve the Body of Christ. For a period of time, he published a renewal magazine that he especially wanted to distribute among Anglicans (Episcopal) where he attended church. He was a solid man.

My last visit with Bill before his death shocked me and provided the reason for this story. We sat at his table for another unusually good meal. (The British are not famous for cuisine.)

"Doctor Bill," I said with mock emphasis, "What is your latest malpractice?"

Ignoring my question, he curtly spouted, "Call me Mister."

I responded, "Have you quit being a doctor or have they kicked you out?"

He silently and intently stared at me while Rene jumped in to explain. "Yes," she said, "In our country, if you have served as a doctor in a long and outstanding manner, they restore to you the title of *Mister*. It is the highest honor."

I sat amazed. When they know you are a doctor, but they call you "Mister," you have reached the highest in your profession. His membership in the Royal College of Surgeons paled in the light of this honor.

"What an excellent illustration of Jesus," I thought. "The Son of God becomes known as the Son of man—the King of kings becomes the Servant of all."

The height and goal of both Bill and Jesus was to be numbered among the transgressors. Some traditions are worth keeping. Now, I just hope someone is keeping the arguments going in heaven.

In the meantime, anyone know a good Mister I can go to?

Discussion:

1. With whom do you have your most fun discussions and what is the usual subject?
2. Have you seen any of your friends highly honored? How did you participate?
3. Do you ever have "friendly" arguments? Over what?

Rhino vs Elephant

The game park behind Bill and Rene MacGowan's house fielded spectacular views of wild animals in their natural habitat. On one viewing platform, we watched a drama unfold that had spiritual implications.

An elephant with a young cow and a rhinoceros were in a clearing together. The rhinoceros, a frustrated female who had no baby in her care, jealously attempted to get between the elephant and her baby and take the little elephant away to be her own.

The activity was intense, but the rhinoceros had two problems to overcome–a furious mother and a determined baby. The rhino had a full-time job keeping the baby elephant away from its mother, because that baby elephant exhibited full determination to get back to mother. The rhino could not give full attention to the baby because she had to also keep a defensive eye out for the mother elephant.

I asked MacGowan who the victor would be in a full-on war between an elephant and a rhinocerous. He said the outcome was uncertain. Either could win, however, they would need full attention to the battle which this rhino could not afford.

As I watched, I thought, "Satan may attempt to get between us and God and pull us away to be his own, but he faces two problems that approach being insurmountable: a furious God and a child determined to get back to its Father."

Discussion:

1. Can you remember how you felt as a child when you were separated from your parents? Describe.
2. When you are away from church and the body of Christ for a while, what is the effect on you?
3. How might Satan most likely try to separate you from God?

Feedback...

I rarely spoke at meetings of a certain large international men's organization. My story and style simply lacked the snap they sought. However, the influence of a pastor for whom I was speaking snagged an invitation to speak at a Saturday breakfast meeting in this state's capitol.

We arrived about twenty minutes early and entered a hall with places set for 150 people. Twenty people were gathered in one corner energetically chatting. The local president and moderator introduced himself to me, welcomed me, then led me to the head table where I would be seated. A small chalkboard stood behind the table–evidence that chalkboard was not the norm for their sessions.

By the time breakfast began, only twenty-five people had arrived–all huddled near the front. Throughout the breakfast, the president, sitting next to me, voiced his disappointment. "I wonder where everyone is? We always fill this room. Why aren't they here today? We advertised this very well. We put your picture in the paper."

I could see where his mind was going as he sought to lay blame for the day. Finally, he asked the question I knew would come: "Tell me just who you are. What is your story?" I responded that I was not really well known. I merely traveled and spoke about the Nature of Jesus.

He stared at me for a few seconds and I could see the decision forming in his mind. He was now convinced that he had booked a loser and something must be done to save the day. He launched a jazz-em-up, dance-the-aisles, make-em-happy time that lasted for one and one-half hours. It was important to make them glad they had come since future attendances at breakfasts were at stake.

I knew what was going on and, frankly, I steamed inside and withered outside. When he finally released me to speak, I decided this would obviously be the only time here for me, and I determined not to let this guy terminate the message.

I spoke for one and one-half hours delivering as entire a basic Nature of Jesus seminar as I could, then sat down. It was noon. Silence.

After an eternity, one of the men spoke up and said, "I guess you would like some feedback, wouldn't you."

I stretched the truth severely and said, "Yes." Actually, I wanted to get out of there fast and erase the memory of the day.

The man continued: "Do you know who I am?"

"No."

"I am the Lieutenant Governor of this state and until two weeks ago, I was running for Governor. But God spoke to my heart and told me to get out of the race, because I did not understand leadership. So I obeyed. Today, I have learned the things I did not understand. Thank you. Would you be willing to share this with our legislature?"

I never saw this man again, and I don't know if he ever ran for governor. I doubt that he did. However, from time to time, I would see small items in national newspapers with his name in the article. His name was always associated with some servant-hearted event or action he was doing for people who could not help themselves.

Governor would have been a step down for such a servant.

Discussion:

1. Have you ever had great things expected from you and you felt that you let people down? Describe.
2. If you had a midlife career change, what might you do?
3. If you could do something good that no one would know about, what would it be?

I Was Your Enemy

The board meeting of the church I served veered from normal discussions of business to the hottest topic of the day–the court trial that soon would begin. "I could never be a juror," one attested. "If I were on that jury, I would hang every one of them. That man they killed was my friend."

They were referring to the federal trial of some KKK men over the firebombing death of a Black leader in our town. Since I had just arrived as pastor, this meeting offered great insight to their hearts and thinking. The ineffectiveness of the state's system of justice brought the federal government in to investigate and then try the accused on less-than-murder civil rights charges in order to gain some justice.

Though it was a common topic of conversation, the embarrassed town cast their glances aside as they watched all the defendants convicted.When the trial was over, the press of life forced the event from my mind. I did not know that trial would revisit me on several occasions, even twenty-five years later.

The whole subject came flowing into consciousness just a few months later.One of the pastors of the city had a radio program that was the best I had ever heard. He taught the Bible with a joy, insight and thoroughness that proved the Author was his best friend. I met the man on numerous occasions and grew to love and respect him. One problem–he was Black. In this town, still racked with KKK influence, friendship with him had some costs.

I spoke of him one Sunday morning in my sermon. After describing him and my respect for him, I told of how I longed to spend time with him and to have him stick his feet under my table, but I knew the atmosphere in the town. "They may burn the parsonage and the church down, and that house and this church building are not mine, they are yours," I stated, "and I have to keep that in mind."

From the front row and the mouth of one of the deacons shot an answer that continues to ring in the halls of my memory: "Pastor, let it burn!"

Shortly after that, I left that town wandering even farther away with memories growing ever dimmer, then, twenty years later, in a flash, everything came back. I was teaching at a missions school in Hawaii when I overheard a tall, wiry student state that he was from that city where I had served twenty years before.

I made my way to him, smiling, to reveal that I once lived there. He asked, "When ... and what did you do?"

"1968 and 1969, pastor," I listed.

"Then I was your enemy," he responded. "I was one of the men convicted for bombing the house of the Black leader killing him. I became a Christian while I was in prison."

After regathering myself from the shock, I told him the stories of my days there. Friday brought our goodbyes until we ran into each other at Chicago O'Hare Airport about two months later.

Five years passed with no further contact or knowledge until another trip to Hawaii for another school. The leader of the school asked me if I hadn't lived in this certain town. With my positive response, he rushed to his office and brought me a book by this man. He said, "I think you will find this book interesting."

Indeed, I could not put the book down as the inside story of KKK activity was revealed. One most interesting development–the author, who now lives under a different name, decided not to turn damaging evidence of KKK activity over to the police, but promised that he would if they ever committed any violence again in that state.

You can hear the quiet.

Discussion:

1. Do you ever distrust the conversion of some-one in prison?
2. Do you think jail is enough price for some crimes or should restitution be made? Why?
3. If you were to sit in jail alone for a year, what changes would you expect in yourself?

A Skull vs Stripes

A summer, like any other summer. 1969. I grew accustomed to emergency calls. Pastors do. This one was intense. The breathless caller informed me that the son of one of my parishioners had lost control of his motorbike on a gravel curve and had flown headfirst into a pole at fifty miles per hour. He was on his way to the hospital where his newly-informed parents were headed also.

I arrived shortly before them and watched as the teenager was unloaded from the ambulance. Blood and mud covered his face which twitched in constant seizures. I feared for his life. By this point, the whole church was being alerted to pray.

The family, once they saw him, returned to the waiting room and sank into a grieving stupor. Comfort has its limits in the absence of information. After praying for them, I wandered back to the X-ray room and watched as they carefully held him rigidly and turned him for X-rays from different angles. The doctors were waiting for the results. My familiarity with the hospital and its small-town casualness gave me much freedom.

I knew where the X-ray viewing room was and quietly walked down the hall toward the door about the time I knew the film would be ready. The door, slightly cracked, permitted all the view I needed. I heard them whistle in disbelief as they placed the film against the lighted viewing plates.

Even from my view, the results were obvious. A split the width of my little finger ran the entire length of his skull from front to back. The doctors became aware of my presence and closed the door. I alerted the parents to what might be coming up.

The doctors took an envelope filled with the film and walked immediately out to the parents. "We are not equipped to do anything for your son," they reported. "We will place him in an ambulance and race him to a much larger hospital (one hundred miles away at the state capital). Hopefully, they can help. We are shorthanded on nurses. We must find one to accompany him."

Finally, a nurse from surgery, a dear family friend, volunteered to ride with him. The father also rode in the ambulance. The mother rode with me as we raced along to keep up with the speeding, flashing lights ahead. The talk was serious, the tears frequent, the anxiety high, the questions many, the prayer constant. Only in our hopes would he live. Then the *stripes* gained control.

How can you explain those moments when you just know something to be true though you have no evidence? I simply knew. I turned to the mother and said, "Your son is OK. He is going to be all right. I just know." She was afraid to hope that much.

Later, the nurse accompanying him could not tell the story without crying. She said that she always wanted to see a miracle but never thought she would be monitoring the pulse when the unbelievable happened. His life signs had been steadily deteriorating as they raced along in the ambulance. She was afraid he would die before they arrived, but suddenly, his pulse and blood pressure stabilized and became normal. She could not explain, because nothing was actually being done for him. She merely was tracking his progress as they traveled.

By the arrival, he was conscious. The doctors checked him in, looked at his X-rays, took new ones, checked his bleeding, looked again and marveled. They said, "You are actually OK. You only have bleeding in the scalp. Except for the fact there is a half-inch gap in your skull, we would send you home. We need to watch you for a while. This is hard for us to believe, since we just sent home as a vegetable a man with just a small skull crack."

We were almost afraid to believe. When I visited him later in the hospital, his eyes, barely able to peek through his swollen face, sparkled. He said, "You know, I even feel smarter, now."

A week later, he came home. Though still summer, we declared the next Sunday to be "Thanksgiving." Applause and praises greeted his entry that Sunday. This was not Turkey Day, this was Thanksgiving! By the way, his grades (miserable until then) greatly improved.

"...he went out to the place of the Skull.... Here they crucified him." John 19:17-18 NIV
"...by his stripes ye were healed." 1 Peter 2:24

Discussion:

1. Describe any experience you have had of God's healing.
2. Have you had a crisis experience that improved your life or attitude? How?
3. What would you like to see God do for you now?

The Fleece

Gideon started the whole controversy. God told him that he would free Israel, and Gideon acted on that information in a way that put him in fatal collision course with the enemy. Then, he suffered pangs of doubt and put a sheepskin on the ground asking God to make it alternately wet and dry, opposite to the nearby ground's condition, so he would know that God had authorized him to do these risky things.

So, we have taken that act of doubt and formulated a whole theology. To "put out a fleece" is common lingo and action. But we have a problem: What constitutes a good fleece, indeed if any fleece is good? Weirdness permeates the genre. For instance, I heard of a man who said, "I'm putting out a fleece. I will know God wants me to divorce my wife and marry my secretary if the sun comes up tomorrow."

Now, everyone recognizes the absurdity of *that* fleece, but here's one that strikes closer to home. Adrian Plaiss speaks, in his hilarious diary, of a fleece that he felt a need to put out in response to a request by his church. They asked him to join them in ministering to the poor in downtown London. He answered something like this: "If, at 4:45 a.m. tomorrow, a man shows up at my door dressed like a Japanese admiral, I will know God wants me to help you."

Sure! Or, even closer to home, the prospective university student, frustrated in making a school choice, makes his fleece, "The next letter I get from a school will be the one you want me to go to." Yes, miserable decision making.

However, I must tell you of a fleece of my own. I planned for years to be a surgeon, but now, as a college freshman in a time of prayer and contemplation, God was offering me another option: preach! I knew it was Him and the whole issue became settled in my heart, then, in a moment of mental weakness, I decided to put out a fleece.

"God, I don't have an automobile, and you know I can't preach without an automobile. (I don't know where it says that in the Bible.) I will know you want me to preach if you supply me with an automobile."

Feeling smug, I returned from my place of prayer to my dormitory. If I had been listening closely, I would have heard God chuckle. One week later, here came my car! You could hear it for a mile. Sounded like the pistons were trying to change holes in midcycle. My father was driving.

Now, you need some additional information. My father had suffered extensive brain damage in an accident twelve years earlier but had retaught himself to drive. Alone, he had driven *my car* 150 miles to this university.

"Son, about a week ago, I had the strongest feeling that you needed a car." I was melting! "I have some friends at a used car lot who tell me this is a good car."

"Friends?" I mentally questioned.

He handed me the keys, then reached into his pocket and handed me the documents. I quickly flipped through them and then stared in disbelief. The payment book! He handed me the payment book! I would never have bought this car, but now it hung around my neck (no, my wallet!) like an albatross.

Fleece, fleece, chuckle, chuckle.

That car tried me. Driving along at night, suddenly all lights would go out. You had to place your feet carefully or they would go through the floor. I had to park the car on hills at night so I could get it rolling fast enough to start in the mornings.

On cold mornings, as I pushed that car, I could hear the Lord chuckling and asking, "Are you going to do that to me again, Gayle?"

"Never!"

"Never?"

"Never!"

Discussion:

1. How do you know when you have heard from God?
2. What methods do you use to verify His voice?
3. Have you ever felt that some method you used to hear from God failed you? Describe.

Twelve Steps

It was a dark and stormy night. OK, OK! Cliché, cliché. But that is exactly what it was. I had gathered two of my parishioners willing to brave the wind and rain and drive to a country church where a denominational gathering would occur.

We arrived before anyone else and the pastor, who lived next door, joined us at the front of the sanctuary just to chat. Time passed and the storm worsened. We paid little attention because of the pure pleasure of the fellowship. Finally we realized...we would be the only ones there...all three of us! We continued our chat with the pastor there on the front pew of the sanctuary.

At 7:30 p.m., the pastor looked at his watch, took the twelve steps up to the pulpit, donned his sanctuary voice and said, "It's time to begin. Get your songbooks, turn to page 230 and let's really sing." We looked at each other and wondered what had happened in those twelve steps that had changed his voice and his manner so dramatically.

Discussion:

1. What do you think causes a "sanctuary tone?"
2. What do you do because it is the "traditional way"?
3. How do you feel around someone who is often in the public eye? Are you surprised if they differ in private?

The Bag Man

I always liked Sunday nights as a pastor. Casualness coupled with fewer time restraints permitted me to teach larger portions of Scripture as we would go through different Bible books. Because of my style of teaching, I usually stood down in front of the platform and near the congregation on Sunday nights as I was doing on this particular occasion. I was about thirty minutes into the teaching when it happened.

From the back door, I watched a man carrying a large paper bag enter and walk steadily down the left aisle of the auditorium to the front row of pews. He sat about twenty feet to my left. Anyone entering that late grabbed everyone's attention, including mine. His paper bag rattled noisily as he shifted around so he could reach the contents.

Our eyes glued to each other as I tried to continue the message, he reached into the bag, pulled out a large knife and laid it on the floor. I watched closely and kept talking, although few, I think, were listening. Then he reached into his bag and pulled out a gun and laid it on the floor beside the knife. Now, he truly had my (no, our) full attention. Then he reached once more into the bag, pulled out a Bible, and laid it on the floor beside the knife and gun.

To continue with this distraction would be pointless. I stopped to talk to him. "I assume this has some meaning," I began.

"Yes. I am trying to decide which one of these I am going to use," he responded. By now, I am thinking more rapidly than usual though not necessarily more clearly. The church elders assured me later that they were prepared to jump to my defense, though I lacked evidence of that at the time.

Somehow, the addition of the Bible and the sheer openness of the situation caused me to realize that he was not a present danger to anyone, so I encouraged him to just sit there and listen as I finished my message and I would be glad to help him decide afterward.

Sure enough, as we talked, the question had to do with danger, not to me, but to himself. We discussed his relationship with God, and he decided to become a Christian.

We let him keep the Bible.

Discussion:

1. Describe some times you felt you were in physical danger.
2. We all have "fight or flight" decisions to make at times. Which one tends to rule for you?
3. What method do you use to avoid conflict?

April May June

*Names and locations are changed in this story
for obvious reasons.*

Her looks as well as her name, April May June,
won her the award of "Calendar Girl" from a
fraternity at the University of Avalon. I knew her,
because her dad (and she) frequented my grandparents' house during the time I lived there. Almost every holiday they would be at our house
during family meals. They seemed to have no
regular home and would occasionally, for extended times, stay with my grandparents.

When my grandfather described April's father
as a man "with a millionaire's brain and a pauper's
bottom," I felt that I had all the information I
needed to understand the situation. My grandparents also numbered as friends a wealthy family
who owned a major manufacturing company.
Their son, Jerry, and I became good friends
though he was about seven years older than my
tender fourteen. I considered him one of the finest
people I had ever met.

April May June liked him, too. Really liked him!
Forgive me, but I could not and can not get my
grandfather's "brain/bottom" comment out of my
mind. April won her prize and she and Jerry were
married. Her wedding dress exceeded the word
finery. These events made it appear that all her

dreams (and perhaps her dad's) were being ful-
filled, until a moment of fateful realization torpe-
doed a fleet of families. The realization? Jerry did
not have access to sufficient family funds!

Not to worry! Funds were in Jerry's father's
wallet, so the focus of amorous attention shifted
to a different bottom, uh, wallet, uh, man. You
may find this hard to believe, but April won Jerry's
father, divorced Jerry and married the father who
had also divorced Jerry's mother in order to complete this little opera. Well, few battles are won
without an exchange of cannon fire, so every form
of lawsuit possible was launched. The newspaper
in the town of Bumberchute had enough front
page material to form legends.

Soon, (You could predict this!) the costs of
litigation and time drove the company and its
owner into bankruptcy. By the time April achieved
her goal, the goal no longer existed. She had
trashed one of the finest persons I had ever met
for an old man who now had nothing. She moved,
with her new and virtually penniless husband, to
California. The only reason I know that is because
the phone rang at my grandfather's house during
a Christmas meal. April's dad was there. The call,
collect for him from April, pled for enough money
to leave California and come back to Bumberchute.

What I learned from watching this event unfold
cannot be properly communicated in this story;
however, the story does not end with this final
phone call. April had no place to keep her personal
treasures including her opulent wedding dress, so

she stored them with my grandparents and finally disappeared, abandoning everything she had.

Years later, when I found Tennessee's best and convinced her to marry me, she had everything to fulfill my dreams for a wife except for one thing: She was as poor as I was. Not wanting to burden our parents, through generosity of friends and special deals, our wedding plans proceeded. But what to do for a dress? Wedding dresses are horribly expensive. Not to worry! My grandmother shipped to us an abandoned dress whose finery exceeded everything in the wedding except the bride, whom it fit perfectly. I think God has a sense of humor.

Discussion:

1. How do you think this situation could have been rescued?
2. Have you ever tried to achieve something and found it to be much less fulfilling than you expected? Can you describe?
3. Would you rather I not have covered the pain of this story with humor? Have you ever been in a painful situation in which you resented attempts at humor? Read the story again and re-tell in your own words.

A Mystical Moment

Serving a small church in a southern town stretched me in many ways. The congregation, composed mostly of very old and very young with few in between, was controlled by the arch-conservative old, since the young go-getters were mostly Air Force personnel whose lives were highly mobile and unsettled.

Amazingly, one young chap from an Army base fifty miles away began hiring a taxi on Sunday mornings and bringing some of his buddies to church. He spoke often and glowingly of his home church on the West Coast. He kept saying, "They would like you at my church. I wish you would visit there."

It so happened that my wife and I were going to a conference on the West Coast, so he gave us his parents' phone number and insisted that I call them. When we arrived, I called and they made the hour-long journey down to see us. We met and chatted in the lobby of the convention center. He, the head deacon of their church, and his wife were anxious to hear reports on their son.

Then the mystical moment happened. As we talked, a thought so strong that it almost took wings and flew out of my mouth—"I'm going to be your pastor some day."

I controlled myself, though, and as we parted, I chuckled at the craziness of such a thought for me, a mere twenty-six-year-old beginner. With hesitation I shared that crazy thought with my wife. She was amused.

We returned to our church to find that the Army fellow had been sent to Vietnam. We would not see him again.Three years later, life moved us to a new location–eastward. My wife and I laughed that we were going the wrong direction if my thoughts were true. Two years later, a dramatic development sent us packing again–to the north. We laughed again. Wrong direction!

Now, on the headquarters staff of a denomination, our minds were dominated by the excitement of creating youth magazines. The West Coast dropped out of our minds. Eight years passed with no further contact with that deacon or the church after the meeting in the lobby.

The main magazine I developed for youth had been greatly successful and I settled into the routine of the office, although every weekend, I was flying off somewhere to speak. On one of those routine days, I sat in my corner office, looking at my commanding view of a parking lot (real prestige, here) when the phone rang. On the line was the deacon I had met eight years earlier. I couldn't believe what I heard.

"We are without a pastor and your name keeps being recommended to us. We think you are the one, so would you come out to speak to us and be interviewed?"

He didn't remember who I was and now he was inviting me to consider being his pastor! The phone seemed to melt in my hand. I agreed to be there one month later.

The church building seated two thousand, but walled-off segments of the auditorium made the 130, mostly elderly people, in attendance look slightly less lost. Two other much more vigorous ethnic churches used the building, which was downtown in a major city. The head deacon voiced strong views against both ethnic groups and I knew my first clash would be with him. I began to shudder.

In the interview, my vision as a pastor fell on unreceptive ears. The three months necessary for me to arrive, though I was willing to fly out and speak each Sunday, seemed like the final straw. The interview didn't exactly close, it just ceased.

Sunday night, I found an alone time and stood in front of the church, looking at the neighborhood, thoroughly confused and praying. "Lord, you know that I will come here if that is what you want, but our hearts are not at all together. If I came, the agony I am feeling would be multiplied by the agony they would feel. So, please don't let this work out unless your kingdom will truly benefit."

I flew home knowing I would probably never hear from them. I didn't. My wife felt that I had probably missed the will of God somehow in my interview. I struggled in my mind to establish a reason for the whole procession of events. My emotions were in some disarray, since I had been so convinced that I would be moving there, that I had released all my current ministry from my heart. Limbo.

Perhaps the release in my heart was the purpose of this long-term drama. I did not know that a large and powerful wave was thundering toward me that a year and a half later would deposit me on the West Coast, ninety minutes away from that church.

The next six years after my visit to that church were filled with my greatest agonies and my greatest ecstasies, with my greatest successes and my greatest failures. All of this punctuated with an occasional question from my wife that maybe I had missed the voice of God by not going to that church.

Near the end of that six years, a rare Sunday free of assignment slid into my schedule. Such an unscheduled Sunday was so unusual that we didn't know what to do. "Honey, I have an idea. Why don't we drive to the church where I interviewed six years ago and see what is happening?" The idea met full approval of the family.

We introduced ourselves to the greeter at the door. No recognition in his eyes. We wanted to be anonymous, but were welcomed and introduced in part of the service. We were still anonymous. No one remembered. The service was identical to six years earlier. They were jubilant in announcing that they had 130 present.

On the way home, my wife put my heart at rest. "Honey, you did the right thing."

From this and other personal events, as well as the observation of others, I have come to deeply distrust the mystical but keep an open mind when it comes to determining the voice of God.

However, when it comes to truly hearing from God and fulfilling His will, nothing beats reading the Bible and making Jesus Style choices.

Discussion:

1. Have you ever had "strong thoughts" or expectations that failed to come about? How did you react?
2. What do you think when someone says, "God told me...?"
3. How would you handle a situation where two or three people said they had heard from God yet each had a different plan or program to present?

Outloved

As I taught one of my college classroom sessions, a brilliant student stated that when he was in high school, he knew every question to ask anyone who tried to witness to him. In fact, he said that he could have anyone doubting their faith inside of thirty minutes.

"So, why are you a Christian, then?" I asked.

"Well," he said, "I joined the Army and at the base where I was stationed there was a group of guys who really loved God and loved each other and loved me. I couldn't resist!"

"But what about those questions?" I replied.

"What questions? Oh, those. Unimportant!" was his answer.

So here was a brilliant person who was not brought to Christ by someone "outbrillianting" him, but simply by some people outloving him.

The leader of the group of Christians at that base is now my son-in-law, Peter Robbins. Am I blessed or am I blessed!

Discussion:

1. How did you come to a relationship with God?
2. If others were involved in bringing you to Jesus, what is your relationship with them today?
3. What do you think is the most effective form of evangelism?

The Professor

L os Angeles to Amsterdam flights last forever, so I sat grateful for the upgrade to business class and grateful for the Powerbook laptop, a gift from some friends, that I was working with during the flight. A man across the aisle noticed my computer and inquired if I had a spare battery. He grinned sheepishly and said he had exhausted his playing games and still needed to work.

I apologized that I didn't have one, but the ice was broken. Later, when I finished and stood up to stretch, we began to talk computers, then life. He was a professor at the University of Southern California and on his way to Holland for a visit. He, of course, asked what I did. "I have more fun than anybody. I travel all over the world teaching on the Nature of Jesus."

"I'm an atheist!" came his curt reply.

"Really? You are really an atheist?"

"Yes."

"Tell me, how did you, a professor at USC, come to the conclusion that there is no God?" I took him by surprise. Probably for the first time he was being asked to justify his disbelief. University systems rarely require you to justify your atheism, only your Christianity. He stumbled for a few seconds, so I continued: "I can't look at the vast-ness of space and the intricacy of a cell without thinking that there must be a designer, a mind behind all of this."

"OK, mister, you've got a point. So, I guess I am an agnostic."

"Well, that's movement, but tell me how you, a professor at USC, came to the conclusion that you cannot know whether there is a God or not."

"Look, mister, I have a system. I believe in life."

"Great! So do I." I knew what he meant by life, so I pressed on. "Do you have a tree at your house?"

"Yes."

"What if I were to come and strip some leaves off your tree? What would you do about that?"

"I would be upset."

"Because it's life, right?"

"Yes."

"But you really wouldn't do anything to me."

"No, I guess not."

"Do you have any children?"

"Yes."

"What if I came and killed one of them? What would you do?"

"Now, that's different!"

"But it is just life. Unless there is different life. Do you have a fireplace?"

"Yes."

"What do you burn in it?"

"Look, mister, I buy it!"

"Ah, so you hire a killer! Are you wearing leather shoes?"

"Yes."

"Killed something for that didn't you?"

108

"Touché, mister."

By this point, the stewardess had moved us twice because of complaints of passengers who wanted to sleep. Now we stood behind the galley and next to the toilets on this 747.

"OK, mister, I'm a seeker. I would love to have what you have, but I don't know how."

He listened to the Gospel carefully, asking questions. Though he did not make a decision at that point, he accepted my card and a copy of *The Jesus Style*.

Even atheists want to know what God is like.

Discussion:

1. What was your most memorable witnessing experience?
2. What intimidates you most about witnessing?
3. To whom would you most like to witness?

Mode and Mary

Ada and I drove, as part of our sentimental journey, to Choctaw Ridge. Perhaps you remember the song that contained the line, "And Billy Joe McAlester jumped off the Tallahatchie bridge." I was baptized in the Tallahatchie River. If Billy Joe jumped off the bridge, he might have sprained an ankle!

That song also speaks of Choctaw Ridge, a place of great and warm memories. My family faced deprivation one winter, not knowing how we would get food. A hillbilly on Choctaw Ridge named Mode Corter heard of our plight and told us that if we were willing to pick them, he had enough beans in his hills for us to eat. We were willing.

Mode and Mary Corter became a joyous part of our lives. Mode was seventy-two years old and could not read or write. He told me that he had gone to school two days in his life. The first day he learned how to court; the second day he learned how to fight; that was all he needed to know, so he quit.

His stories were a delight, but his actions were hilarious. About every six months, he would don his best clothes (He never wore shoes unless he came to town or church.) and head into town for a day. He loved the dime store. He would find a place to sit and simply watch people and the store all day long. Some who came in thought him to be a salesman or the manager of the store. He duly explained different items to help people make decisions though he knew nothing about what he was doing. Job hunters would see him and, assuming him to be the manager, apply for a job. He would listen, ask certain questions, then tell them they were just who he was looking for and to report to work on Monday. By Monday he was safely back up on the Ridge. Chaos!

One story might have been true, but stretched my ability to believe just a bit. Mary was only twelve when he married her (true) and could not cook (true). Mode reports that he bought a month's supply of cooking materials, locked her in the kitchen and told her not to come out until she could cook (maybe). If she failed with a batch on her wood stove, she was to throw it out the window to the hogs and start again (perhaps). Whether that happened or not, Mary was a world-class cook (true).

I wanted to take their picture with my rudimentary, flashless camera so it had to be done outside. Mode called the hogs, against the protest of Mary, so they could be in the picture, too.

"We are hillbillies, Mary, and the picture will look more natural if the hogs are there."

There was life in "them thar hills."

Discussion:

1. Who do you know that you would call a "colorful" personality? What makes them colorful?
2. If you have ever had a time of financial deprivation, how in that circumstance did you see the hand of God?
3. Do Mode and Mary meet your definition of hillbillies? Where have you found stereotypes (such as "yankee" or "southerner" or "country boy") to be inaccurate?

Dirty Pictures

Like many other rides to airports or next stops, my driver (an old friend) and I talked of many things, dissecting life and meaning. We rejoiced in each other's company after years of not seeing each other.

The conversation shifted, as it often does, to an area of need and growth. "I have a problem, a decision I need to make and maybe you can help me." Hardly a trip goes by without hearing those words.

However, unshockable me was a bit unprepared for what I was about to hear. "I have some pictures at my house that I'm thinking God might want me to get rid of," My friend blurted out. "I have had them for a while but now I am becoming concerned about what would happen if some people saw them. I know it would damage how they see me and I might not be able to minister to them properly if they see them."

Mixed emotions flooded my soul. Could my friend not see clearly what was being said? Was there any question, really, about the removal of the pictures? What could I now say?

Before I could respond, my friend continued. "I know this is a lust problem for me and I need to do something about it. I certainly don't get any satisfaction from them. What do you think I should do?" Squirming a bit, I struggled to stay cool and calm, hoping that simple logic might handle the situation.

"Did God tell you to put these pictures up?"

"No, but God didn't tell me to put up the pictures of my mom and dad, either."

"But God hasn't convicted you about the pictures of mom and dad."

"True."

"But he is speaking to you about these other pictures."

"Yes."

"There has to be more to this," I thought, so I pursued the question. "Why would you put them up in the first place?"

"Well, they do represent some power to me. They do symbolize challenges and successful conquest."

"Wouldn't you rather let God reward you as a victor and conqueror than to look at and remember this?"

I knew that my friend was single and the pressures of life could be unbearable at times, but I hoped the conviction being felt would produce some sort of repentance.

We drove on. Thoughts swirled thick enough to cut with a knife. Occasionally, my friend would just say, "Hmm. It is so difficult. I just don't know."

Finally, hesitantly, the thoughts and questions found completion. The victory was won. My friend went home and took her pictures down–the one with her posed beside a former president as he signed a bill, the one with her standing by a

Supreme Court Justice, the one with her and a famous performer.

The lust to be seen with famous and powerful people had been conquered. She only wanted to be known because of her relationship with Jesus.

Discussion:

1. Would you ever consider publicity or "seen with famous people" photos to be "dirty" pictures?
2. How does someone's image affect how you relate to them?
3. What types of photos would you expect God to convict you about?

Childcare

When Valerie came home from school, crisis procedures took over. As a gentle third-grader in a new town, she and we trusted the walk from our house to the school and back. That turned out to be a mistake. She arrived crying and beaten up from the attack of a gang of kids. A quick investigation caused us to believe that this was a once-only event, so we comforted her and sent her back to school the next day.

On the way home, the same thing happened again. That was it! This is my daughter and they were not going to treat my daughter that way. So, for a week, I walked her to school and then walked her back home. I wanted all the neighborhood to see who her daddy was and who they would have to hit several times before they got to her again.

Before I left each day, I would look in the mirror and practice looking mean. On the way I would scowl at everyone we met. I took along the "Gayle Erwin nonviolent threatening system," my camera. Whenever we met anyone, I would ask her, "Is that one of them?" If she said, "Yes," then I would point my camera and click the shutter. The shock of being recognized would register on their faces. They now knew they could not hide in anonymity. They were on permanent record–like the great memory of God. Actually, I had no film in the camera. Not necessary.

From then on, she walked in peace. They knew her daddy and they knew her daddy knew them. Enough.

Discussion:

1. Describe how you have seen the protective hand of God. When do you pray for his protection?
2. How do you think God might be protecting you when you are not aware?
3. How do you think God wants us to view his other children? Do you have difficulty doing this?

Diedre

Every breath seemed like the last to Diedre's heaving little body. Minutes earlier she entered the breathing world weeks too early. Doctors quickly assessed the situation, and Diedre's first day of birth began with six hours on the operating table as surgeons attempted to close the multiple large holes in her left lung.

Finally, they closed her chest. The little form lay too small, the lungs too delicate, the holes too many and too large. The doctors informed her parents that they had been unsuccessful. All they could do was leave a tube in her chest in hopes that they could drain the leaking air fast enough to keep the lung inflated, which, to this point, had not worked. These events occupied all of Saturday and by Sunday morning doctors' hopes had faded. However, Diedre's parents and friends hoped in a different source for her.

At about 11:00 on Sunday morning, the people of Diedre's church were praying for her. They knew that any healing could not be argued. Any miracle would only glorify God. At about 11:00 a.m., the holes suddenly closed in Diedre's lungs.

Though premature, she was now a healthy child. In the following months as she would go for her checkups, all the personnel of the clinic would gather to observe the miracle child and wonder at the fact that her left lung was stronger than her right one.

Discussion:

1. Have you ever seen a miracle of healing? If so, describe.
2. Describe any other sort of miracle you have observed and any reactions.
3. When did you last join a large number of people to pray for a single thing? What need brought you together in prayer?

Blackouts

Pascagoula (yes, where the squirrel went ber-serk...) is a Gulf Coast shipbuilding town, which, during World War II made it a prime target and a defense town. German U-Boats hovered just off the coast. Camouflaged gun emplacements lined the treed shoreline. Frequent gun target practice would rattle the windows of the whole city.

As a five-year-old, I was both excited and terrified. The top half of all automobile headlights were painted black to keep enemy planes from seeing the lights at night and thus knowing where to drop bombs. I checked the skies frequently.

The blackout was the most terrifying of all the precautions. Often, at night, loud sirens would sound. Citizens of the city were to go home and turn out all lights in and around their house. The city must be shrouded in darkness to foil enemy attempts to bomb. Five-year-olds don't under-stand this, but one other item made it almost unbearable.

Whenever people sat together in the dark of a blackout, they whispered when they talked. To me, that meant that the enemy was in our yard and we didn't want them to hear us talking. The only relief available would be the next siren signal to turn the lights back on.

Ah, light!

Discussion:

1. What special fears can you remember from your childhood?
2. What do you consider to be your greatest external threat?
3. What fears do you battle the most now?

The Playground

Traveling west out of Urbana into downtown Champaign, Illinois, you pass under a railroad trestle out into a large brick plaza where several streets emerge. Behind my van as I approached the underpass followed a large truck and a car.

Beyond the underpass, I noticed a small girl running out into the apparently empty plaza. To her it looked like the largest playground she had ever seen. I knew that the truck behind me could not see her or avoid her, so I took the only steps available.

I slammed on the brakes while under the railroad, effectively blocking the road, jumped out of my van and ran to retrieve the little girl. The truck and car drivers who also had to do an emergency stop were honking and shouting obscenities at me.

I ran to the little girl, who, when she saw me, began running, terrified, away from me. I picked her up as she screamed and pushed me away. The vehicles had backed up to come around the underpass and the drivers continued their abuse as they drove by.

As I held the screaming baby girl, I knew her mother must be somewhere nearby. Sure enough, a distraught mother rounded the corner of a building, spotted us and began running toward us.

At this point, there were no other vehicles or people around, only me and the screaming baby girl trying to push away from me. The mother rushed up in a huff, grabbed her daughter as she scowled at me and began to walk off. A few steps away, she stopped, looked back at me as if to say, "You pervert!" then stomped on off. Nothing was said by either of us.

I stood there for a moment and simply felt the situation. Everyone was mad at me–the vehicle drivers, the little girl, the girl's mother–yet I had just saved the little girl's life. I walked numbly back to my van where other vehicles were now taking evasive action.

Just before I began to seriously feel sorry for myself, the Lord impressed on my heart, "Now, you know how I feel most of the time."

Discussion:

1. Have you ever had your actions totally misunderstood? How?
2. When have you been upset with God because you thought He might have failed you?
3. How and from what do you tend to most want to rescue people?

The CEO

I sank gratefully into my first-class seat, thankful for an upgrade from my frequent flying. Often, passengers retreat to their own thoughts, but the chap next to me chose to verbalize his. He was high up in a major corporation and on his way to a trouble-shooting task.

Soon, we talked of life and travel. The discovery of my massive miles and hours and countries brought the expected question: "Just what do you do, Mister?"

I answered as I usually do, "I have more fun than anybody. I go all over the world teaching on the Nature of Jesus."

"I'm not a religious man myself," he shot back.

"Really? Then where do you get your values?"

"What do you mean? I just have them."

"Well, values are given or imposed when we accept some authority. No one automatically has values. Someone must give us values. If you don't believe in God and the Bible, how would I know what you value?"

"I guess you wouldn't, but I want to earn enough money to be secure and raise my family right."

"But if money is your value system, if I did business with you, you would probably cheat me."

(Pause) "Yes, I guess I would."

"So, if you aren't a believer in the Bible, you have no trustworthy, predictable value system."

"Well, it's all so complicated. Who is right? It's too complicated for me to figure out."

"That's strange. I know children who have figured it out."

"OK, OK. But I'm a busy man and things are going good for me. I don't have time for that."

"Well, everything has a price, and at some point, you won't be busy and things won't be going good. In your system, you are headed for destruction and you have nowhere to turn. How will your money help you if one of your children dies..., or if you die?"

He stared at me silently. I continued. "Look at it this way. Suppose you are right and I am wrong. I am not rich, but I am having so much fun I can hardly stand it. I harm no one, I eat and sleep well. If you are right, tell me what have I lost?"

"Nothing!"

"But if I am right and you refuse to know and serve God, what have you lost?"

His response was quick, "Everything!"

We had come to the gate and the door of the plane was about to open. Only then did I realize that our conversation was heard all over our first class cabin and that the people silently listened.

I offered him my card and asked him to call me. He took the card and bade me goodby. A quiet, thoughtful group exited the plane.

Discussion:

1. In your observation, what are the main reasons people give for not being a Christian.
2. Describe some of your own values and relate how you received them.
3. If you could sit in my place on the plane, what would you like to tell this CEO?

Trophies

Every person collects trophies. Whether you are conscious of your trophies or not, they line the walls of your heart and maybe your house. I collect trophies, too–nothing that I have *won*, mind you, but some things I never want to give up. They represent victories in a way far more important than any competitive sport. These are trophies of life that come because the Kingdom of God is winning. Let me describe a few.

The Armband

The "Hitler" of Romania, Ceaucescu, had been overthrown for only four months when I made my second journey to that country. Accompanied by Damien Kyle, I made my way to the town of Brasov in the center of the country at the foot of the Transylvanian Mountains to teach a group of young people and see what the Lord was doing among them. The week was cold and difficult, mostly because I was not over a virus that still caused hoarseness and uncontrollable coughing, but the hearts of the young people were open and responsive.

At the end of the week, they marched out some gifts from them to us. Two of them gave specific gifts that continue to be displayed in my home and my heart. During the Romanian revolution people gathered en masse in the downtown plazas to protest the government and display their unity. Each person would wear an armband of the colors of the flag to identify himself as a protester. This act subjected them to machine-gun fire of the Secret Police. It was an act of bravery.

One of those armbands now graces my home. I see it daily and pray for Romania. A true trophy.

The Cloth Case

India possesses so many stories that I barely listened to Joy Punnose as he told me of a Burmese pastor who, working alone, founded about twenty churches under the most difficult circumstances in Burma (now Myanmar). Times became so hard and persecution so difficult that he despaired about his churches and their pastors. Somehow, (This is not clear in my memory.) he heard that an organization in India called Gospel for Asia helped support such pastors. With a minimum of information and no money, he set out on a gigantic journey by foot, bus and train making his way by selling cloth side bags he had made.

After a month of journeying he made his way to the headquarters of Gospel for Asia in Kerala State on the Southern tip of India. He knew none of the Malayalam language of Kerala or even Hindi or English, the other main languages. When he arrived, he could not communicate who he was or why he came. They considered him to be a beggar common to the area and sent him elsewhere.

He came back each day, growing weaker from hunger, when finally they realized that something more was present in this man. By the sign languages instinctively created by people, they learned where he was from, managed to find someone who knew a little of his language and began the relationship that would result in the support of his pastors. His persistence and bravery was remarkable.

The last of his cloth bags, his personal one, hangs on my wall–a continuous invitation to prayer for Myanmar and a gentle reminder of the ease of my own life.

Suspenders (if you are an American)
Braces (if you are British)
Hosentrager (if you are German)

I happen to dislike wearing belts. (Please resist the temptation to comment about my body shape.) When suspenders came into style, I was delighted and determined to keep them in style. For me, they were the most comfortable way to hold my trousers up hitchlessly.

Alas, they have become my trademark, and by gift and design a rather bright (sometimes wild) part of my wardrobe. Some I bought because they were outrageous, others are trophies.

One pair is rather bland until you look closer and notice that against its grayness are the signatures of about forty-five people who expressed their love to me after a week of teaching by wanting me to wear their names. That trophy now hangs on the wall of a Christian coffee house on the island of Maui in Hawaii.

The Giant Pen

The very computer on which this is being written is a trophy. Frankly, I'm a gadgeteer delighted by the invention of the computer. It surpasses all other tools or machines I have owned in saving time and doing the difficult. In early days, *Servant Quarters* took me two weeks to type, copy fit and paste up. Now, all can be done in one morning. Also, I work best and think best typing rather than handwriting. (A chorus of "amens" arise from all who have seen my handwriting.)

Therefore, logic says that to enhance my writing as I travel, I needed a notebook computer. To my delight, friends of mine were thinking ahead of that. A group of them got together and from their generous hearts presented to me the Macintosh Powerbook that I am typing on at this moment at 32,000 feet over New Mexico. Now, am I blessed or am I blessed? This is a trophy that displays itself to me almost every day.

The Stock Certificates

My grandfather, a very astute farmer whom God always prospered (That is a story in itself that I must tell you some day.), at one point, owned some stock in a major automobile manufacturer in the infancy of the automobile. Because he didn't think the automobile, as he observed it, was going to make it, he sold the stock. Mistake!

My father learned from the mistake of his father, so when the Tucker automobile came out, he sank his life savings into that company.(You don't know what a *Tucker* is? That is the very problem.) The stock certificate was passed along to me for the fun of it since I was with my father in that crowd on the day that the Tucker was introduced to the world. It is an interesting trophy. Add to that a model Tucker automobile given to me by Earl Pitts of Canada. At least it reminds me that this world is not my home.

The Pot

Zimbabwe, formerly Rhodesia, has been a favorite country of mine for many years. Many events associated with my visits warm my heart regularly. Once, when Ada and I visited, people wanted us to visit their houses and walk into every room then pray for them. They believed that blessing would flow to every room we were in. I was amused, but deeply moved.

At the home of a black lady who was the best translator I have ever had (She could translate into Shona simultaneously while I was speaking.), she came with a pot in her hands running up to our car as we were about to leave. She handed the pot to us explaining that this had been in her family for many years having been made by her grandmother. She wanted to give it to us.

You will see that trophy when you visit us, but don't miss what is inside. Oh, it's nothing dramatic; just an old, ragged, white towel. The towel, too, is a gift. I found Black Zimbabweans to be very generous with us though they had virtually nothing. (They averaged about $35 a month in income.) After speaking at churches or conferences, they would take up offerings for us, mostly composed of small coins with an occasional $2 bill. They gave generously out of their nothingness. Often, they would have no money at all, but moved by their own hearts, would give whatever they had.

Money cannot be taken out of Zimbabwe, so we spent or gave away whatever we received while there; however, ragged white towels given as a widow's mite can be brought home. A trophy that only we can understand.

The Bronze Head

In 1978, I made my first trip to Southern Africa to what was then Rhodesia. I had been invited to speak at a National Renewal Conference–only the second conference of any sort in the country to which all races had been invited. I was honored and gladly paid the cost from a poverty college teaching salary to get there.

They chose to give me a very heavy teaching load including several hours on Christian family subjects that resulted in more hours spent talking to individuals and smaller groups. It seemed that the nation had never had a chance to explore the subject or face a counselor. One such person whose life began to come together during the conference happened to be an accomplished professional artist. She indicated that she wanted to give me a gift, but I routinely discouraged it.

Finally, she insisted that I come to where her car was parked and decide if I wanted to receive the gift. There, wrapped in cloth in the seat was a museum-quality life-size bronze sculpting of the head of a Shona tribesman. Nothing could have been more appropriate for me. I had come to deeply love the people of the country. No symbol could have been better.

If you visit me, you will find this sculpture prominently displayed. I see it and I think of Zimbabwe, and pray for its people. On subsequent trips, I met people who used the tapes of those sessions as "church" during the difficult days of their civil war when travel was severely restricted. I think of those people and cherish the trophy.

The Photos

A special drawer holds photographs. Some are the children of dear friends. Other pictures are from people who have adopted me as their grandfather (or dad). One is even a "snap snap" shot (private joke here). Some (most?) are pictures of me in various indignities while I am speaking. (I could never run for president with these photos in evidence.) Many are pictures of people who have chosen to pray for me. Some are from people who want me to pray for them.

Pot Pourri

So many other trophies adorn our house and office that it is impossible to tell each story. They range from suspenders especially made for me (Aloha!), pottery especially made for us, Gayle dolls (?), paintings, caricatures and other forms of art, letters, Calorie Chapel memorabilia, tapes, CD's, food (that adorns something else) such as chocolate covered raisins, jalapeño peppers and salsa. Life is such a gift of gifts.

I wonder if anyone in the world has such a collection of trophies from people who love you and who let you know. I doubt it. Maybe I should open a "museum of the heart."

Discussion:

1. Describe the trophies or special mementos that you have.
2. Which ones did you earn and how and which ones were gifts and why?
3. If you could give someone a special trophy, to whom would it go and what would it be?

Galena and Zeneida

The unusually large crowd at the Jordan River site, where Christian Pilgrims often are baptized to commemorate the baptism of Jesus, gathered and stared over the railing as several pastors immersed their parishioners. I knew these were mostly Romanians who had come to work in Israel as well as some scattered other Eastern European workers. I was glad they were watching. They were very quiet and respectful when we were having the service. In fact, the only people who disturbed our time were western tourists who insisted on getting in the middle of things to have their picture taken without regard to what was happening.

I baptized, at the end of the progression, those people who wanted to be immersed and whose pastor was not along on the trip. I considered the opportunity a joy and privilege.

The water, not as cold as I remembered in prior winters, seemed to increase the number being baptized. Just as I finished my statement and lowered the last person in the symbolic death, I looked up and saw two more people coming into line dressed in white robes. I did not recognize either of them.

They approached me as if they knew exactly what they were doing and stood ready to be baptized. I was surprised, but glad to serve them. When asked, the first lady blurted out her name.

"Galena from Russia," she proudly declared. I announced her name and country to the crowd and they applauded vigorously.

After baptizing her, the next lady waded closer and I asked her name. "Zeneida from Brataslava," came her reply. My own heart was thrilled that I could be present at this great moment for these ladies. They waded back out of the water and I followed. Zeneida stopped at the edge of the river, leaned against the wall and wept. I waited near her to share her great moment.

The baptismal session was over. They disappeared back into the crowd. I may never meet them again, but I was glad that I was there and that they were.

Discussion:

1. When and where were you baptized?
2. What meaning did baptism have to you? What other spiritual experiences have meaning for you?
3. How would you feel about being baptized in a strange place surrounded by a crowd of unbelievers and tourists?

Venice

Most people think that the Mississippi River ends at New Orleans. They are surprised to discover that another one hundred miles stretches, then meanders to the Gulf of Mexico. The isolated, little-known delta land served varied and often questionable purposes in its past. Not until the 1940's did the engineers build a road toward the mouth. Until then, only boats could take you to this area.

For that reason, many who wanted to disappear from the world–escapees, malcontents, hermits–found a life that pleased and protected them far away from governmental eyes. The census could only guess at the number of people living in the marshland and among the bayous. Business was "cash only" in this area.

In most parts of the parish (as Louisiana calls its counties) addresses didn't exist. One simply hunted until he found the house he was looking for.

My arrival there to serve my first pastorate is still a source of wonder. My wife and I thought we were going to East Tennessee to serve a church there, but though the call from that church was made in the form of a letter, we did not receive it, so we found our way to this remote spot.

The church had been without a pastor for nine months. Their mortgage payments were behind to an embarrassment. Places to live were scarce and very low quality. Work was plentiful, which was good for me since the church was unable to help a pastor in any way. The whole area sat on a pool of oil, so most of the work revolved around the oil industry with fishing taking the remainder. Actually, most oil workers involved themselves with fishing also.

First Sunday Eye-opener

The area operated as if it were a colony of old "apartheid" South Africa. Three separate school systems existed for whites, blacks and mulattos, those who were a mixture. How your birth certificate described your race had total control over your life. Evidence of the overwhelming racism captured our first two Sundays there.

Church service ended near noon and an hour later, I received a call from one of the two deacons in the congregation. He had been involved in an accident near his home and asked me to come and see to his affairs while he took his family to the hospital. I was not prepared for what I was about to experience.

The deacon had been hit by the car of a black man as he was pushing to get it started on a narrow blind lane. I arrived shortly before the sheriff's deputy. (There were no incorporated towns in the parish, so the sheriff's department handled all policing details.)

The first words out of the mouth of the deputy were (Forgive my use of them, I am only reporting.), "Nigger. You got any insurance?"

"Naw Suh."

"You know they can put you under the jail for this, don't you?"

"Yassuh!"

"Now, it won't help you for this accident, but if they know you have some, they might go easy on you. I can sell it to you now."

"Yassuh."

The deputy whipped out an application pad, filled it out, collected his money and then said, "OK, now tell me what happened here."

I sat there quietly wondering what kind of place God had sent me to and what my role would be. I didn't know that the next Sunday would provide even more evidence.

Once again, service had ended and all the folks were gone. As I prepared to lock the doors, I looked up the highway and noticed a number of cars gathered, precariously parked along the elevated road. Wanting to explore anything exciting in our new area, my wife and I jumped into our car and drove up there. As we slowly drove by, we asked the people standing around what was going on. No one would tell us, nor even say anything to us for that matter.

The parish had no newspapers, so we knew this would not be a news item. We returned to our house frustrated. However, our landlady served as the area *human* newspaper and she filled us in on all the details. A black man had caught his brother with his wife and shot and killed him. He was arrested and taken away, simple as that. Three years later, it occurred to me to ask our landlady what had happened to the man who had killed his brother. She informed me that he was still working for the administration at the county (parish) seat and as long as he worked for them they promised they wouldn't hang him. Slavery still existed.

The county was governed, no, ruled, by a man who had no official position in the county government. He was merely chairman of the advisory council to the elected officials. He so totally dictated that even PTA committees in schools would not offer any reports until they had checked with The Administration as they called him.

Passing Failure

After working for an oil company for two years in order to be able to pastor there (The church paid no salary.), I finally landed my original goal–a job as a school teacher. A few weeks after my work began, I received a phone call from a neighbor, a party hack for The Administration.

"You're being paid by The Administration now and I see you are not registered to vote. You need to register so you can help The Administration out when they need you."

"I haven't registered because I didn't want to get involved in politics here. I only wanted to help people in spiritual ways."

"I don't care why you came here. You have to register because we are paying your salary." (My salary, by the way, was $3000 per year.)

"I can't register. The office is open only during the week and I have to teach at that time."

"They will be open this Saturday. You be there."

Ada and I drove up the river road and took the ferry across to the parish seat. Nothing was open except the office to register to vote. The official waited, feet on his desk, for us to arrive. He handed each of us a test on the constitution which we had to pass before we could register. Suddenly, I had a brilliant idea. Since I had extensively debated this constitutional subject while in high school, I knew which answers were wrong. I purposely failed the test. I nearly laughed when the official informed me that I had passed.

Then he asked with which party we wanted to register. I told him that I was neither a Democrat nor a Republican. Could I register as an independent? He stared at us for a minute and said, "I guess you can if you want to." We did.

We returned home feeling a small sense of victory that we could register as independents. That sense was shortlived. On Monday morning, the phone rang early. It was the party hack. He screamed at me, "You registered as an independent! Why did you do that? You know you can't help The Administration that way. There aren't any independents down here. You are in trouble."

I reported all this to the school principal where I now taught. He told me not to worry. He would protect me. However, from that time until we left for another pastorate, we received regular death threats by phone.

Black Gold

Who owned the land in this parish was a question that floated somewhere up there in airy-fairy land. This confusion served the greedy well. Fraudulent land seekers would claim land and offer to lease it to the oil companies as theirs. The oil companies, prisoner to the system in place, would pay.

The manager of an oil field supply company told me that when the company decided to open a shop there, he found a vacant place and taped a notice to the door saying he would be present on a certain day to deal on a contract. When the day came, five people showed up with titles to the property. The supply company manager told me, "We looked them over, decided which one looked best to us and have been paying rent to that person ever since."

The oysters in those coastal waters were the largest and best I have ever tasted. Local oyster fishermen would claim oyster leases from the parish government. By law, these one- or two-acre plots of water were to be basically square, but most of them seemed to be one foot wide and about fifty miles long. Here is why. Whenever an oil company needed to run a pipeline from its wells to the storage area, they had to pay for any damage done as they went through an area as well as leasing the land. If an oil company passed through an oyster lease, they had to pay the fisherman for any loss of oysters in his lease.

Now, imagine a series of parallel, one-foot-wide oyster leases running up and down the coastline. To run a pipeline, you must cross each one of them. One company official complained to me that he bought an entire crop for each lease he crossed. It was the only time I ever observed someone getting the best of an oil company. Having been gouged by artificial gasoline prices, I feel justified in applauding these wiley Cajuns.

Just in case you may have forgotten, "Cajun" is an adulteration of the word "Acadian," who were French refugees from the British takeover of Canada. Longfellow made the story famous in his poem, "Evangeline."

Mosquitos, Snakes and Fish

Our first few weeks at the church were difficult, because I had not found a job and we needed to stay alive. The abundance of the area sustained us. I could walk in almost any direction for two hundred yards and fish as much as I wanted...no, I should say catch as much as I wanted. The place was awesome. Plus, we had commercial fishermen in the church who would supply us with fish they could not sell. We ate gourmet.

Yes, I have a fish story and it isn't anything like you think. But first, let me tell you about the mosquitos. One almost needed a shotgun to handle them. They were large and they were plentiful. They ruled everyone's lives. You could not walk through tall grass or stand still in a slight breeze or sit placidly in the cool of the evening outside your house. These bloodsucking machines owned the outside and redefined the word "miserable." As you walked they clung to your clothing and your skin. Slapping each one was like trying to eradicate roaches with a Mexican hat dance. If you were foolhardy enough to just walk along, you needed a grass or horse-tail whip to constantly slap your body, just as horses do.

This mosquito problem deeply affected church and hospitality. Whenever people came to church, they did not simply walk in the door. They would quickly enter in clumps, then stand inside the door and wait while an usher would spray them down with a pump spray can of insecticide. (What a greeting!) We had to kill all mosquitos or they would drive you crazy while you sat inside during the service. The same ritual would happen if people visited you at your house. People came in quickly when you opened the door and then waited while you sprayed them.

The last ritual of any night at our house involved the mosquito. After sucking your blood, they tended to fly to the walls and rest. I rolled up a magazine each evening and walked through the house on a mosquito hunt, slapping them against the wall. Our house was covered with blood spots as if we regularly had violent fights.

Once, somehow, a hoard of mosquitos invaded the house. The ceiling was black with them. My wife took the vacuum cleaner and went row by row and vacuumed them away. Our daughter Angela was extremely allergic to their bites and would scream and claw herself especially at night when they bit. We had to seek a medical specialist for treatment of her "raw" skin.

Let's go from mosquitos to snakes: All four species of poisonous snakes abounded in that area. The last few miles of highway before the end of the road split through a large marsh. Snakes were almost always on the road, even in winter, but in the spring, snake carcasses paved the road from cars running over them. In spite of that abundance, I never heard of any worker being bitten as he worked in the wetlands among them. What an interesting place!

Ultimate Snake Story

Now that we are on snakes, let me tell you the fish story. I warn that you may hesitate to believe what I am about to tell, but the story is true. Sherwood Brine can verify it. He was with me, or I was with him, and he saw and participated in every bit of the incident. We were fishing with gill nets in the back canals of an oil company at the very end of the road. At certain points, small hills rose beside the canals where dredges dumped the refuse as they dug the canals. We picked a corner of a canal by one such hill and slowly released the net into the water. We would then beat the side of the boat to drive fish toward the net. We had only begun to beat the boat when we looked up and saw hundreds of cottonmouth water moccasin snakes writhing in what appeared to be a mating dance.

Most were on the shore and up the small hill but many moved about with their heads sticking out high above the water in this dance movement.

We had large oars and decided to clip off a few heads with them, but as we rowed among the snakes, we realized that we were on their turf and quickly cranked up the outboard and got out of there. Now, I frequently watch nature films and see many strange things in them, but I had never seen any such thing in any nature presentation until just recently, some thirty years later. A naturalist crawled into a rattlesnake den and filmed them in just such a dance, although, to my surprise, I learned that it was not a mating dance at all, but was bull moccasin snakes fighting over who would get to mate with the females. Amazing.

Every Man Has A Fish Story

Indulge me for one more fish story. I loved going to the mouth of one Mississippi River pass, where the water became shallow over mud flats, and fish there for flounder. Well, not exactly fish, gig (a broom handle with a sharp spike on the end) for flounder. You had to have at least two people, three was better. One would hold a bright lantern while the other walked along carrying the gig, looking for the outline of a nesting flounder in the sand. You would then jab the gig into the fish, hold it down while it threw water and sand all over you. (A five-pounder or more could nearly drown you.) Then, you would slip your hand under the fish holding it to the base of the gig and lift it into a game bag hanging at your side.

All well and good except for one bit of excitement. Sting rays, which have a similar shape to the flounder, also nested where the flounder were, and if you stepped on one of them, your trip ended. Occasionally, we would step on a nesting flounder whose camouflage escaped our attention. For an agonizing moment as the earth quaked under your feet, you waited to see if a sharp pain signaled your worst fears. You would think that the raised tail of the sting ray would give him away, but the reeds growing in the water looked amazingly all like sting ray tails.

We never stepped on a sting ray, since the way around that was not to actually walk, but to shuffle your feet along. This would drive away any fish that you didn't actually see, including sting rays.

Moving Up

We left Venice at the invitation of the state denominational leader to come and serve the church he attended in the center of the state. The Venice church had grown enough that the new pastor who came did not need an outside job to serve as pastor. I was very happy about that, however, two successive events turned my happiness into grief.

A year or so after we left, a hurricane ripped through that area destroying almost everything in its path. The church building was demolished. The parsonage we had built was moved a quarter of a mile away from its foundation. The parsonage was moved back and placed on a new foundation. The church was rebuilt, this time of brick.

Not long after that, another, more vicious, hurricane ground the area to mud. Neither the brick church nor the parsonage were ever found. The baptistry was found a half-mile away. I visited the site and realized that the only thing left of my sojourn in Venice was memories.

Discussion:

1. Being as honest as you can, what racial injustices have you observed?
2. What tragedies have hit you or your family and how did they affect you?
3. Because of changes or demolition, what places in your past are only memories to you? What kind of memories?

Baked Beans and Beer

Leonard, a true cowboy, worked on a West Texas ranch. He was only twenty at the time and had recently made a commitment to Jesus Christ, however it was not too deep or too intense a spiritual life he led. Now, he sat on a railroad tie laid near the chuckwagon, exhausted from the morning's work of herding six hundred head of cattle. He spooned his baked beans and drank tea from a peach can.

A photographer happened to be on the ranch that day and he asked Leonard if he minded having his picture taken. "It's OK with me as long as you don't keep me from eating my beans," he answered. For three days, the photographer trailed the cowboy crew snapping pictures along the way. A few months later, Leonard received a form to sign releasing the photographer to use the photos and offering $250.

Struggling to pay debts, including medical bills that piled up for his wife and newborn son, Leonard thought, "$250 would make a hospital payment." He quickly signed and mailed the release.

Three years passed and the photographer session was forgotten. In the meantime, during a visit of a famous evangelist, Leonard fully committed himself to the Lord.

Then, one day, a fellow worker told him that his picture was in bars all over town under the title "Baked Beans and Beer." He then discovered that the photographer had been commissioned by a major company to paint a series of cowboy pictures. In using Leonard, he had replaced the peach can of tea with a can of beer.

The picture was plastered all over the United States. Leonard was crushed. He felt that his new life in Christ was ruined, that he would now become a detriment to the kingdom and his witness would be destroyed. He spent considerable time explaining to people that he didn't know this photo would be used that way.

Turn It Over To Me

Shortly afterward, at the closing invitation of the large Baptist church he attended, he began to sob uncontrollably. God whispered to him, "Are you willing to turn that picture over to me? If so, respond to this call." He lurched to the front, continuing to weep intensely. He felt that he owed an explanation to the pastor, so he went to him and told him what was happening. The pastor asked him to tell the whole church that night, and between sobs the story spilled out. What he did not know until years later was that his story dramatically changed the lives of many people there. They realized the value of their lives and names and the vulnerability of their commitment.

People everywhere began to recognize him and ask if he was the cowboy in the painting. This opened opportunities to tell about his new life in Christ. Many came to know the Lord. God was doing a good job with the picture under His care.

His new deep relationship with the Lord took him to the Calvary Chapel Bible School at Twin Peaks, California and then on to a seminary degree from Southwestern in Ft. Worth. After seminary he and Jan and their two sons, Justin and Tell, moved to Nebraska to pioneer a Baptist church. He hoped that no one would know him and that the painting would not be a detriment.

His anonymity lasted only a few hours. Every bar in town had his picture on its wall. Soon, a reporter came from Omaha and did a story on him that hit the front page of a major Omaha newspaper under the title (slightly erroneously, since he had only briefly carried a pistol to protect himself from marijuana growers in the outer ranges) "Cowboy Trades Pistol for Pulpit."

Crowds came to church to hear and see this remarkable story. Conversions were the order of the day. One very old couple drove from Iowa just to hear him speak, then, at his questioning, revealed that they were not Christians but wanted to be. They became!

Because of what was happening, his home church began massive assistance to help them build a church. After eighteen months, they had a building paid for and full of people. But his heart was in Midland, Texas and they soon left to go back home and plant a church.

However, his plans were intercepted by an invitation to return to Twin Peaks Bible College, this time as a teacher. After a stint there, the pull of Midland grew too strong and he returned to begin what is now Country Chapel. The very people he would most want to reach already know him. They see his picture every time they visit a bar in the city. And they wonder. Some find out. But Leonard is not the only one in his family with a story of the grace of God. Jan has a story, too.

Jan's Story

Jan's mother committed suicide when Jan was eighteen years old. The date of that death, March 20, haunted her for years. She hated spring because March 20 was coming. This day became the opposite of a holiday, a day of depression and pain. The loss revisited her annually, refusing to let her cope with the grief.

You Must Abort

Marriage helped but did not heal the hurt. Soon a child was on the way in their house, however her body reacted so violently to the pregnancy that she had to seek medical help for that sickness alone. Her doctor declared that this sickness was psychological, that her body was trying to reject the fetus and she should have an abortion.

Unsatisfied with this diagnosis, they went to another doctor who also declared the condition to be psychological and urged her to get an abortion. A third and a fourth doctor gave identical advice. In their discouragement, they began to actually consider that option, painful as it was to them. Her violent sickness continued, reducing her hunger and adding to her malnutrition. They decided to try one more doctor. He examined her more closely and discovered a vitamin B deficiency and gave her a shot. As they left, she told her husband that she was ravenously hungry. They promptly went for a steak. Her sickness was over.

When the baby was delivered, the doctor handed Justin to Leonard and said, "This is the baby that four doctors told you to abort."

Ah, but I am ahead of myself in this story. God had designed this moment for multiple victory. Justin was due in early February. When the day arrived, no indications of birth were forthcoming. Since everything was healthy otherwise, the doctor said, let's just wait. Days and weeks rolled by. Jan fretted that this baby was getting too close to March 20. The last thing she wanted was for the baby to be born on such a day of pain.

Her distress increased until, sure enough, a remarkable six-week-late baby was born to them on March 20. She complained to God and others that this would happen, until she realized that her mourning had now been turned into joy by her newborn. Gone was the pain and grief. God had used this baby Justin as a double victory.

Awesome.

Just about the time you think you have heard it all, God's Grace shows itself again and I return to the realization that I am a walking mass of ignorance gleefully awaiting His next show of power–the kind of power shown in Leonard and Jan Cotten.

Discussion:

1. Describe any experience in which God took what you thought was a mistake and used it for good.
2. Describe a time when you stood up for what was right though everyone seemed against you.
3. Describe any symbols God has given you to signal that past hurts are healed.

Stories Yet Unwritten

An incomplete list of people who have blessed us.

Benny, Eldon, Lyle, Cindy, Callie, Vanessa, Ouida, Brandon, Jared, Gladys, Agnes, Angela, Winsome, Faye, Guillermo, Cameron, Myrtis, Julianne, Naomi, Estelle, Cora, Cherie, Dottie, Arch, Marsha, Jake, Kirk, Lindsay, Miles, Marshall, Vonna, Mickie, Adam, Renate, Laurel, Rolf, Margy, Cass, Wendel, Eliane, Eunor, Dudley, Neva, Hattie, Nita, Powell, Leona, Sergio, Woody,

Ollie May, Darnell, Irma, Alison, Burt, Oli, Noah, Josie, Elaine, Honey, Tommy, Sean, Eleanor, Daisy, Tros, Tilford, Jean, Ivy, Trish, Happy, Doris, Patsy, Lafe, Toby, Verlyn, Leen, Graham, Sparky, Will, Louene, Ria, Graeme, Zack, Yoshio, Anton, Danielle, Doon, Juan, Cosima, Gabi, Donovan, Jamie, Milo, Vi, Noleen, Priscilla, Brenton, Travis, Sheridan, Marnie, Deanna, Catorce,

Pacheco, Clem, Butch, Ludmil, Webster, Jacob, Rosalind, Felix, Grady, Howard, Mable, Loren, Randy, Sylvia, Carleton, Clara, Abigail, Melba, Milton, Duff, Simon, Mae, Hazel, Patty, Felipe, Dana, Coralea, Bernard, Snow, Talo, Allene, Edna, Gigi, Lucille, Wilfred, Sonny, Neels, Kayla, Merle, Arlene, Lew, Honor, Sabina, Petria, Jo, Kevin, Roberta, Lane, Martha, Carlton, Edmund, Hal, Sheila, Hans, Russell, Dominick, Jennifer, Rose, Lance, Dawn, Marjorie, Rob, Lowell, Kathee,

Vince, Carla, Gudrun, Marvin, Sheila, Jerry, Shaun, Cliff, Darwin, Connie, Marc, Carlos, Lavelle, Andrea, Ellen, Merrit, Alfredo, Laverne, Bernice, Ethel, Jan, Lucy, Romaine, Lenora, Hilda, Darold, Mary Ann, Madeline, Tillie, Myron, Clarke, Trevor, Grace, Ramona, Fernando, Allen, Grant, Gib, Shelly, Gayle, Leonard, Shirley, Teresa, Lauren, Ada, Erin, Eileen, Kaye, Brett,

Wendy, Troy, Mario, Cynthia, Reuben, Jorge, Louis, Marcia, Cecil, Jose, Tonya, Les, Kimberly, Vergil, Michelle, Lon, Kai, Alejandro, Charmine, Judy, Carol, Stacy, Helen, Brant, Clare, Fern, Stacie, Ethyl, Claudia, Leota, JoAnn, Sharon, Mary Lou, Rillis, Rita, Charlotte, Virginia, Lisa, Willard, Inga-Lill, Bert, Tina, Kerry, Melvin, Lynne, Bobbie, Kari, Evan, Teri, Joshua, Chad,

Rhonda, Judith, Sandra, Gina, Laurie, Lawrence, Blake, Carlin, Joel, Anna, Laurence, Eva, Ford, Ann, Elizabeth, Nathan, Ruby, Cecilia, Monica, Beth, Vivian, Robin, Kelly, Al, Thomas, Logan, Randall, Jeanette, Danny, Brad, Razz, Trina, Paula, Drew, Alan, I.G., C. G., Christy, James, Garry, Carl, Jody, Gerry, Kent, Glenda, Winston, Fausto, Fidel, June, J.M., Augustine, Glenn, Chip, Matt, J.C., Wynn, Moises, Monte, Kristy, Lynn, Monty, Herman, Joe, Dino, Neal, Darrell,

Gertrude, Frances, Aurelio, Leo, Guinn, Hank, Doug, Bernie, Jaca, Ed, Katie, Wes, Rommel, Derald, Malcolm, Marco, Darren, Isidoro, Mandy, Willie, Shannon, Vic, Daryl, Raul, Ginger, Neil, Clark, Xavier, Lafayette, Alvin, Andy, Jackie, Rich, Craig, Marilyn, Joy, K.P., Jay, Trent, Marge, Gisela,

Gene, Chico, Buzz, Rick, Dwight, Jerel, Dane, Betty, Huck, Guy, Richie, Shawn, Lee, Derrell, Oden, Carlos, Wilce, Rubel, Daniel, Jeb, Rodney, Roger, Curt, Fred, Gino, Florence, Sanford,

Liz, Manuel, Pancho, Ben, Lloyd, Joyce, Manual, Kin, Danita, William, Louie, Claude, Tony, Stanley, Vicki, Arthur, Bil, Karen, Stan, Rosemary, Jack, John, Steve, Mary, Tom, Myrna, Marlene, Phil, Pauline, Cathy, Laura, Wynetta, Dagma, Donna, Ralph, Terry, Paul, Clyde, Sheri, Bruce, Nancy, Ezekiel, Hallie, Charles, Gail, Kay, Brenda, Terri, Dot, Sandy, Ron, Timothy, Hugh, Kim, Debra, Skip, Aaron, Debbie, Cassandra, Taryn, Zachary, Dora, Imelda, Isaac, Josh,

Kazuko, Lola, Marissa, Ollie, Ryan, Tim, Peggy, Casey, Donald, Lonnie, Valerie, Amy, Mikki, Gordon, Marian, Barbara, Jon, Erika, Jill, Ken, Tammi, Whitney, Henry, Wayne, Pat, Diane, Austin, Damian, Kathy, Bonnie, Geoff, Greg, Jordan, Bill, Bret, Jeff, Annie, Peter, Chuck, Rene, Jane, Keith, Scott, Gloria, Jesse, Sam, Michael, Kris, Harriet, Duane, Justin, Mike, Murray, Pierce, Brian, Chris, Vera, Coralie, Jessica, Nick, Frank, Jaime, Gillett, Pam, Mick, Dave, Larry, Nelson, Victoria, Colin, Gilbert, Karin, Jeri, Harold, Roby, Maureen, Linda, Marty, Elma, Janet,

Dale, George, Gary, Rod, Dempster, Earl, Gordy, Dorothy, Bob, Bev, Andrew, Renee, Julie, Denise, Mark, Sue, Charlene, Saria, Raymond, Cheryl, Dennis, Erlene, Richard, Deborah, Gus, Becky, Lenya, Charlote, Joseph, Ray, Dee, Millie, Charissa, Dean, Gracie, Spud, Ian, Daren, Jerrod,

Maggie, Maurice, Iris, Luke, Flo, Gil, Ernie, Cranford, Maxine, Zeke, Tyler, Lorna, Joanna, Harley, Mel, Ty, Gabriella, Lois, Francois, Amber, Alma, Edith, Britanny, Gaylen,

LaDon, Lilly, Oscar, Darla, Walter, Darlene, Ross, Fabian, Elsie, Worth, Natalie, Luigi, Kyle, Justus, Holly, Buddy, Naleen, Odie Vee, Lori, Suk, Kathryn, Sonia, Dallas, Damaris, Henrietta, Clayton, Ted, Bud, Julius, Roy, Min, Francisco, Noel, Vern, Floyd, Yolanda, Boyd, Doc, Yvonne, Glenna, Emily, Garth, Wade, Joan, Virginia, Gidget, Reggie, Emil, Tammy, Rocky, Leland, Crystal, Georgia, Lorraine, Jereme, Mona, Heather, Faith, Paulette, Edwin, Norman, Shonda, Nolan, Rusty, Dominic, Reg, Jayne, Carolyn, A.J., Wally, Shelby, Melody, Johnny, Chet, Wilma,

Bessie, Stephano, Buster, Hollis, G.V., Edwina, Shane, Dorel, Deano, Mitchell, Madge, Armando, Virgil, Tiffany, Sophia, Shana, Sidney, Gareth, Rudy, Hector, Garrett, Byron, Lavon, Vernon, Todd, Max, Silas, Jason, Curtis, May, Shaw, Van, Miyo, Leta, Jonathan, Roxanne, Miriam, Wendell, Inez, Gerald, Hannah, Angel, Penny, Eugene, Bracy, Audrey, Arnold, Carey, Alex, Melissa, Leroy, Walter, B.L., Harvey, Sidlow, Julio, Alice, Pedro, Christian, Stephanie, Irene,

Flora, Doreen, Isabel, Fuller, Clay, Lester, Regina, Melinda, Wanda, Aubrey, Loretta, Brent, Delmar, Otis, Ruth, Sheldon, Deyon, Warren, Barbie, Annette, Bethany, Hugh Lynn, Tracy, Beatrice, Johnese, Starlen, Billie, Thelma, Patti, Cory, Char, Keila, Miko, Barry, Norma, Evelyn,

Wolfgang, Anita, Eunice, Heidi, April, Carmen, Stuart, Lanny, Kerek, Allan, Stewart, Forrest,

Regan, Anthony, Dustin, Patricia, Megan, Rex, Esther, Rachel, Birdie, Katherine, Susan, Royce, Kazuo, Harry, Jenny, Jenna, Russ, Keiko, Gwen, Aan-Sofie, Cathleen, Janell, Kasey, Herbert, Blair, Leah, Ira, Cosmo, Candice, Luann, Del, Nicole, Nelda, Charlie, Hodding, Len, Olga, Brady, Fran, Phyllis.

Heaven is going to be a fun place.

Other Books by Gayle D. Erwin

The Jesus Style

This book, now in more than twelve languages, has been featured by Guidepost, Family Bookshelf and Word Book clubs, used as a training manual in many churches, a textbook in colleges and seminaries, and a "book of choice" for reference and for giving to others. First published in 1983. In 1997 its 40th printing. Yashua Publishing, Box 219, Cathedral City, CA 92235, paperback, complete with study guide, 225 pages. Audiobook available.

The Father Style

This book breaks new ground in studying the nature of God the Father from the perspective of the Nature of Jesus. After reading this book, you will be able to love God with all your "heart, soul, mind and strength." Yashua Publishing, Box 219, Cathedral City, CA 92235, paperback, 203 pages. Audiobook available.

The Spirit Style

Approaching the Holy Spirit through the prophecies and life of Jesus, this book heals and resolves many of the events and positions that create conflicts in the church. Yashua Publishing, Box 219, Cathedral City, CA 92235, paperback, 220 pages. Audiobook available.

Resources to complement the books written by Gayle Erwin

Video and Audio Tapes

Forty tapes cover the basic themes of *The Jesus Style*, *The Father Style* and *The Spirit Style* as well as other passages of Scripture. Appropriate for all ages. Additional tape sets are available on The Gospels (16 tapes), Israel (4 tapes), A Couples' Retreat (4 tapes), Conducting a Home Fellowship (4 tapes), The Holy Spirit (10 tapes).

Message Shirts

Sweat shirts and T-shirts are uniquely and beautifully designed and contain the condensed message of each book. Available in many sizes.

Servant Quarters

This magazine/newsletter is sent free six times a year to those who ask. It contains the latest writing and teaching materials of Gayle Erwin and others, responses to radio and writing ministry and news.

To order, contact:
Servant Quarters,
PO Box 219
Cathedral City, CA 92235
Phones:
Voice 760-321-0077   Fax 760-202-1139

Gayle Erwin has spent forty years as a pastor, college teacher, evangelist and magazine creator and editor. He devotes his time now to teaching and writing about the nature of Jesus.